NEXT GEN LEADERSHIP

NEXT GEN LEADERSHIP

SECRETS TO SUCCESS FOR FUTURE LEADERS

HUNTER TIEDEMANN

NEW DEGREE PRESS

NEXT GEN LEADERSHIP

Secrets to Success for Future Leaders

ISBN 978-1-64137-149-0 *Paperback*

978-1-64137-150-6 *Ebook*

For Nomi and Jess Hunter and Trudy, Doris, and Alfred Floyd Tiedemann, the best leaders I have known, yet never met. I carry your names with honor, respect, responsibility, and gratitude.

For Evan, Laurie, and Bob Tiedemann, the best expressions of lead by example.

CONTENTS

"A true leader has the confidence to stand alone, the courage to make tough decisions, and the compassion to listen to the needs of others. He does not set out to be a leader, but becomes one by the equality of his actions and the integrity of his intent."

—US ARMY GENERAL DOUGLAS MACARTHUR

INTRODUCTION

"The greatest leader is not necessarily the one who does the greatest things. He is the one who gets the people to do the greatest things."

—RONALD REAGAN

Jimmy Fitzgerald's team moved into position during one of their highest stakes missions yet—search and rescue. The team had approximately two hours to find an injured mountain biker trapped deep in a remote, mountainside forest. Speed, precision, and focus were paramount as the clock ticked away on their chance to save the victim.

Each member of the twelve-person squad was a steely-eyed, devoted team player with fierce loyalty to Jimmy. Such deep-seated loyalty had been earned as Jimmy lives by the creed that "People only follow leaders who can first lead themselves." Jimmy had consistently proven to his teammates and higher leadership his ability to plan missions, assign roles, stay calm under pressure, communicate, and support his teammates. His teammates respected, trusted, and admired Jimmy for these traits and their collective buy-in to Jimmy's leadership made the difference in the field.

Every member of the twelve-person team received their role in the pre-mission brief, varying from navigation to medicine to communication with headquarters. Jimmy had prepared for these missions vigorously in training, planning for every contingency and scenario. However, once the call to commence an operation came, Jimmy was hands-off, granting his team the freedom to execute their roles to the best of their expertise.

The victim was located in a distant, treacherous part of the mountain beyond the capabilities of available assets. The team would need to insert about two miles away, further down the mountain, then find their way up to the victim. Shortly after inserting and gathering their bearings, the team's two navigators were up first. Using their GPS devices and compasses, the navigators directed the patrol toward the target. They relied on flawless communication with the team's radio man to relay the terrain on the ground to headquarters and find the easiest route to the victim. Jimmy assigned these teammates their roles for their exceptional performance in training and everyone trusted them to execute their jobs well in the field.

Forty-five minutes after insertion, Fitzgerald's team encountered a serious problem. As the team moved further up the mountain, a dense fog began to permeate the forest canopy. Navigation became practically impossible as the fog severely limited visibility. Disorientation and fear of getting lost quickly set in on the team. The situation was quickly becoming dire as the victim's life was in danger and there would be no excuse for failure.

As precious time ticked away with the target lying hopelessly on the forest floor, Jimmy pulled the unit together to reassess and prioritize, recentralizing command when the mission seemed to be disintegrating. Maintaining his composure, Jimmy calmly instructed the team to think back to their pre-mission brief and their commander's intent. Intelligence suggested the victim was located somewhere in a five-acre rectangle marked by four enormous boulders at the corners. If they could just find one of these landmarks, they could locate and save the victim.

Jimmy's teammates rose to the occasion through Jimmy's example. One can imagine the fear and isolation operating in a remote, foggy forest with no help nearby. But the team followed Jimmy's lead and refocused on the mission, pushing those fears and distractions out of their minds. The team's navigators paused to collect their surroundings, communicate with headquarters, and relocate the most direct route to the target area, using intermediate landmarks to navigate the confusing, foggy forest. Jimmy stepped aside again, allowing the navigators to take the team's reins. They backtracked for several minutes and located one of the boulders next to a tall tree, a key landmark indicating they had entered the five-acre area destined to hold the victim.

Sensing time was running low, Jimmy assumed leadership again and ordered the team—whether medical, navigation, or communications—to organize into teams of four, spread out across the coordinates of their target area, and scan east to west for their victim. The team had no problem following Jimmy's orders because they knew how well he had prepared for contingencies on this mission and every other that they had accomplished. Suddenly, a teammate on the first scout team located the victim next to a fallen tree. He came over the radio saying urgently, yet calmly:

"I got him! He's immobile near an oak with injuries to lower extremities."

The medics rushed to the scene with confidence in their skills and determination in their eyes. Despite the early difficulties in the mission, their teammates had pushed on and found the victim and they felt a heightened duty to execute their role. The victim had a broken left leg and right wrist. Now over an hour into the mission, the medics worked quickly while the rest of the team provided communication with headquarters and preparation for extraction, just as they had rehearsed in training.

"I'll address the injury to the left leg," one medic said.

Another communicated calmly, "I need the stretcher and a splint to stabilize the spine, neck, and arm."

One teammate pieced together their collapsible stretcher while another prepared the splint for the victim's wrist. The radio personnel communicated their position to headquarters, estimating the time it would take to get back down for timely extraction. Meanwhile, the medics exhibited perfectly coordinated teamwork and communication, relaying their assessments, plans, and actions to one another as they worked to save the injured man.

Phenomenal poise and teamwork saved the victim's life. Only, the victim's life was never in danger.

The victim actually turned out to be a dummy, placed in the New Hampshire woods just beyond Dartmouth College's football field by Dartmouth's Assistant Athletic Director for Leadership and retired US Army Ranger, Steven Spaulding. Jimmy Fitzgerald was the quarterback of the football team and his search and rescue team was actually a mixture of men and women from several of Dartmouth's varsity sports teams. This search and rescue mission was one of several experiential exercises student athletes complete in summertime during "Drive," Dartmouth's signature leadership development curriculum for varsity athletes.

Jimmy is a remarkable leader and a personal friend, an influencer we should all strive to emulate. Not only did he lead his teammates on many leadership development missions in the New Hampshire forest that summer before football season, he did it after two ACL injuries in the previous seasons. Even though this mission was entirely simulated and Jimmy's football career is now over, he continues to defy the stereotype that millennials just aren't cut out to lead.

He exemplified leadership in this exercise and many others, earning trust first through self-leadership, establishing a vision for mission success, utilizing feedback from his teammates, and working to serve them in support of the end goal during every step of the mission. Oh, and he also founded an undergraduate real estate development fund and earned cum laude status all before he can legally have a beer.

How did Jimmy do this? He followed the model we've developed in this book to help millennials go from commencement to the C-Suite using authentic, people-centered leadership.

Leadership is often associated with fame, power, money, and status. If I asked you to think of great leaders, chances are you would give me someone who is famous, rich, or senior in their organization. When you think of the word "leader," you start to think about titles—CEO, president, general, executive director, or manager. Perhaps you even start to think about famous heroics such as those of Mike Eruzione in the 1980 Winter Olympics, Abby Wambach in the 2011 World Cup, or Winston Churchill in the fall of 1940. Simply put, we have come to conceive of leadership as a platform and not a practice.

But instead of thinking about leadership in terms of title, I want us to start thinking about leadership in terms of behavior. The reality is that certain behaviors were eminent in great leaders before they ever became famous as leaders. No one knew about Mike Eruzione in the fall of 1979, but by February of 1980, he was a national hero and sensation.

However, you can be sure his teammates knew how much of a self-leader he was with heart, vision, and discipline from day one of fall practice in 1979. In essence, leadership is earned before the lights are on and the game starts. People chose to grant their followership to exceptional leaders long before the media and Hollywood got to them.

Increasingly, leadership involves working across generational boundaries, and as it turns out, millennials already possess some great habits that translate well into leadership. In fact, a Workplace Trends study discovered that 91 percent of millennials want to have a leadership role within their company.[1] This is a great start as there will be an immense need for effective leadership from millennials.

The United States economy will be facing a leadership crisis in the coming decades both qualitatively and quantitatively. To begin, roughly ten thousand baby boomers reach retirement age every day, leading to the estimate that 46 percent, almost half of the workforce, will be millennials by 2020 according to researchers at the University of North Carolina.[23] Given these figures, millennials will be in high demand to assume

---

1 "The Millennial Leadership Survey," Workplace Trends. July 20 2015.

2 Russell Heimlich, "Baby Boomers Retire," Pew Research Center. December 29 2010.

3 Jessica Brack and Kip Kelly, "Maximizing Millennials in the Work Place," University of North Carolina Kenan-Flagler Business School: Executive Development. 2012.

leadership roles in their jobs and teams as time progresses. The most important thing to keep in mind is that this time will come sooner than you think. In fact, according to the Brandon Hall Group's State of Leadership Development Survey, while 15 percent of millennials hold management roles today, that figure is forecasted to double in the next 10 years.[4] It's imperative that we prepare to excel in these roles now because the time is fast approaching and the business world needs us.

Not only do we see a numeric need for leadership development among millennials, but we also see the need for a more effective approach. Only 19 percent of organizations say that their leaders effectively meet business goals and only 18 percent say their leaders effectively develop other leaders.[5] An astounding 84 percent of organizations surveyed say that they are expecting a shortage of capable leaders in the next five years.[6] These figures are certainly alarming both in terms of performance and lost potential in failing to develop teammates. I believe the numbers may be slightly overstated as the demands on leaders have grown exponentially with the lightning speed and competitiveness of today's business world. However, it is still unacceptable that over three quarters of

---

4 "State of Leadership Development 2015: The Time to Act is Now," Brandon Hall Group.

5 Ibid.

6 Ibid.

organizations surveyed in this exhaustive report say their leaders are ineffective at meeting goals and growing their people. What are leaders for if not for achieving goals and building their people?

Who is going to fill this gaping hole in effective leadership that drives the next major wave of growth and innovation?

You, me, and the rest of us who are under the age of thirty. Not to worry, leaders of all ages will benefit from this book too.

This book offers a window into how we'll train, coach and build the Jimmy Fitzgeralds of the future. Each of the ten chapters of this book introduces a new leadership concept. Each chapter builds on the previous leadership concepts to develop a dynamic approach to creating high performance teams. For example, communication was integral in Jimmy's mission, but it's difficult to communicate if your people do not believe in your culture. Furthermore, it's practically impossible to receive and utilize feedback if your people are not receptive to your vision as a leader.

The best way to use this book is as a step-by-step guide. Take a few minutes after each chapter to consider how what you have just learned builds upon previous chapters and what you can do to improve in each individual area. This process is like compounding interest—gains in any of the ten facets just raise the tide even more in the other areas.

The lessons within this book are not meant to reinvent the wheel, but rather serve as a rediscovery of the leadership lessons today's leaders wish they knew at our age. While many impressive leaders have shared stories and lessons they learned in the business, government, nonprofit, and military worlds for this project, I have also included peer-reviewed research from top management faculty to support our claims. After months of research, interviews, and real world experience, I have determined that the following ten concepts will provide the strongest criteria for leadership among the next generation of leaders:

- Self-Leadership
- Vision
- Culture
- People
- Service
- Feedback
- Communication
- Don't Push, Pull
- Live Your Values
- Vulnerability

To lead people who have grown up in this new world, and to become a leader yourself, you'll need to apply these ten concepts. This book offers a unique look at how and why.

Not only do we have a leadership shortage, but also the few millennials who are being developed as leaders are learning an outdated school of thought—what I term Leadership 1.0—where status, wealth, heroics, and title mark one as a leader.

The concept of leadership should focus on the followers and the team, not the leaders themselves. The whole concept of leadership is that you do not create the team's success, but rather help orient the team toward success. Furthermore, millennials are significantly different from previous generations in terms of their capacity for emotional intelligence, heightened social awareness, and desire for meaning and accomplishment. In fact, millennials show some remarkable differences from their more experienced managers. When asked to determine what is the most important factor in career success, 30 percent of millennials say meaningful work compared to just 12 percent of managers.[7] Furthermore, only 28 percent of millennials say high pay determines career success, compared with 50 percent of managers.[8]

---

7 Ibid.

8 Ibid.

These figures illustrate that millennials and younger leaders have dramatically different priorities in their careers than their counterparts in older generations. I believe the millennial desire for meaningful work and a sense of accomplishment before high pay is a tremendous asset in leadership because connecting your team to a greater, meaningful purpose should be the foundation of our leadership in today's world. However, too often we hear about leaders who constantly hinder rather than promote their team through egocentrism, micromanagement, and lack of emotional awareness toward their team.

If you're like me, you have struggled with this problem too. One day, our generation will lead the business, government, and military worlds, but how are we to prepare for this moment? How can we be great leaders when all we hear in popular culture is that we are unmotivated, instantly gratified, overly emotional beings? On top of this, I didn't have incredible academic or athletic ability, good looks, or popularity. However, I was an incredibly motivated, disciplined, compassionate kid and it earned me leadership status, Cum Laude Society membership, the Dean's List, several baseball awards, and a chance to study at Georgetown University. You see, the problem in my thinking wasn't that I was lacking those attributes. The problem was that I was thinking those gifts mattered at all.

Leadership is the power to influence and inspire people, not to show off. Sure, it helps to be athletically or academically gifted, but motivation, discipline, and compassion are far more important. I learned to lead by using the attributes I could control, namely my attitude, discipline, and compassion to connect to people. After six years of working on talented teams in the Georgetown University Credit Union, Georgetown Opportunities for Leadership Development, and high school baseball, I started to piece together the way that exceptional leaders build and lead high performance teams. But, one question remained. How do we use these ten integral lessons to fill this leadership gap that is rapidly growing in the business world?

That's the motivation for this book— to transmit these lessons to a generation that the world needs to succeed. After interviewing more than fifty expert leadership consultants, military officers, CEOs, former White House officials, and everyone in between, I am here to put leadership into millennial form so you can take your team to the next level. Not to worry if you are not a millennial because these leadership lessons will be applicable to leaders of all ages.

This book is for anyone like me who has felt challenged with the way leadership is conceived. If you are like me and do not fit the old model of being either exceptionally famous, wealthy, or smart, this book will coach you on how you can take the baton as millennials become the business and world leaders of tomorrow.

Not only will this book impart many influential leadership lessons, but over the course of my months of research and interviews, I have discovered that most leadership lessons are also meaningful life lessons. You'll hear leadership lessons and stories from:

- Co-founder of Priceline.com, Jeff Hoffman
- Co-founder of Rotten Tomatoes, Patrick Lee
- CEO of Goodwill Southern California and Former CEO of the 2015 Los Angeles Special Olympics, Patrick McClenahan
- Former Los Angeles Kings Owner, Joe Cohen
- CMO of the Anaheim Ducks, Aaron Teats
- Former Global Vice President of Branding, Strategy, and Innovation of Godiva Chocolatier, Rich Keller
- Inc. Top 100 Leadership Speaker, Author, and Consultant, Julie Winkle Giulioni
- Leadership Author, Consultant, and Speaker, Karin Hurt
- Co-founder of Blue Circle Leadership, former CEO of Gilt Edge Pictures, and former CEO of New Wave Entertainment, Allen Haines
- Former CEO of Radica Games and world-renowned leadership speaker, Bob Davids

- Former Aide to President Reagan and Chief of Staff to Nancy Reagan, James Rosebush
- Founder and CEO of Headbands of Hope, Jess Ekstrom
- C-Suite Executives in Banking, Finance, and Consulting, Consumer Goods, and Professional Sports
- United States Marine Corps Officers
- Serial Entrepreneurs
- Various Leadership Consultants and Executive Coaches
- College students like me

I hope the lessons of this book serve you well not only for your benefit, but because your team needs you and we all need you. Whether you're a baby boomer or a millennial, if you're ready to become the best leader you can be, join me and let's lead.

CHAPTER 1

SELF-LEADERSHIP

"I believe the choice to be excellent begins with aligning your thoughts and words with the intention to require more of yourself."

—OPRAH WINFREY

"If you are good at discouraging yourself, you can't be a good leader because leadership is built on inspiring others to face challenges."

—ISRAELMORE AYIVOR

Why do we even need leaders to begin with? It seems that every day there is a new headline about leaders causing problems, breaking codes of conduct, or shirking responsibility and sound ethics. Even more often, we hear about the typical bad bosses in our daily lives: the micromanagers, the wild cards, or the "my way or the highways." Over the course of this project, I heard many complaints about the micromanager boss who, as one young woman put it, "Just wouldn't get off my back." If we constantly hear negative press about these individuals, what's the purpose for them in organizations? The answer may seem simple, but it provides practical guidance for how one should approach leading a team.

We need leaders because we have tasks so tremendously large and complex that one person alone cannot accomplish them. Problem solved—we just need to bring on more people to help. In reality, by doing so, we are trading one problem for another. While we have solved the problem of lack of knowledge, time, and other resources, we have lost the uniform vision, commitment, and will of that one original person. Now, that collective vision, commitment, and will is spread among the various members of the newly formed team.

The new problem is not a lack of knowledge, time, and other resources, but a lack of consistency and shared purpose across the team. This is the problem leaders must aim to solve with their work, and it requires just as much EQ, emotional intelligence, as it does IQ, raw intelligence.[9] To spread the

---

9 Sarah Landrum. "Millennials and the Resurgence of Emotional Intelligence," *Forbes*. April 17 2017.

consistency and shared purpose of that one individual across the team, leaders must first gain the trust and buy-in from their teammates. Self-leadership is the path to trust, loyalty, and buy-in from your teammates.

Jimmy's first words to me in our interview were, "No one is willing to follow someone who cannot first lead himself."

If you can't walk the talk and lead by example, you just can't lead. People who can't lead by example will resort to less effective means such as micromanagement. When teammates are micromanaged, they spend more time focusing on how they can avoid being reprimanded and less time focusing on how to win. In essence, when leaders micromanage, people focus on saving themselves instead of saving the team. It takes self-leadership and discipline to earn a team's trust and following rather than assume it through title.

Jimmy would earn his team's trust through his self-leadership in the early days of training. Self-leadership is the all-encompassing commitment to discipline, integrity, and excellence in the face of distractions and excuses. When his teammates showed up to team workouts, Jimmy was the first one there and never cut a corner. When it came time to learn the playbook, Jimmy's teammates turned to him for help. When it came time for study hall, everyone knew where Jimmy would be. When it came time to plan an experiential exercise, his teammates entered the pre-mission brief with a full-fledged plan for success on the table. The overall objective and purpose behind that exercise was transmitted, roles were assigned with the proper training, and communication channels were set up for feedback. Simply put, everyone on the team knew Jimmy had done his homework.

This is the recipe for success in gaining influence as a leader, and it's one with which millennials in particular can win. Show you can lead a team of people by first showing you can lead yourself exceptionally well. If you cannot lead yourself, the one person you have complete control over, how can you expect to lead a team of other independent people? Remember, people follow examples and actions, not words.

Over the course of this project, I had the honor of interviewing several United States Marine Corps officers. First Lieutenant Peter Cohen, who leads sixty operations and maintenance Marines at Camp Pendleton, taught me about his approach to leading by example.

He summed up self-leadership through six simple words:

"Marine Corps officers have tough weekends."

He could tell I was confused, but his next words clearly illuminated self-leadership and leading by example:

"We have tough weekends because the Marine Corps holds officers to a very high standard. If you go out on the weekend and do something stupid, they're going to throw the book at you. How can you expect your Marines to follow your standards when you can't follow them yourself?"

Lieutenant Cohen understood that the best teams are created by leaders who understand that their example is always being watched, whether the lights are on or off. People are drawn to leaders who make them feel secure and confident in their team's goal. What creates that aura of security and confidence in a team is the assurance that their leader squares away their responsibilities, sets their own bar high, and holds themselves to that standard.

Lieutenant Cohen continued with his best insight yet, adding, "It's an honor and a privilege to lead Marines. And they deserve the best, which means you are expected to be able to outrun and outperform them."

On top of consistently setting the right example and instilling confidence in your team, self-leadership tames the tendency to relish in the privileges of leadership. How often do we hear about the lavish salaries, perks, and extended vacations of leaders? Perks and privileges for leadership are fine and deserved, but the problem arises when leaders use those material enticements for their ego. Those amenities are for your title, not for you as a person. Most importantly, people don't follow and become inspired by titles, but by leaders with character and vision. The best way to combat the indulgence of ego through perks and privileges is to consistently adhere to high standards of self-leadership and set the example for effort and enthusiasm.

One doesn't even need to formally be in a position of leadership to excel through self-leadership. If you're like me, entering your final two years of college and looking to enter the workforce, chances are that we will not see a formal management position in the near future. However, this should not be a reason to neglect leadership training, but rather a reason to practice leadership even more. If you'll allow me, I think a personal story will illustrate this well.

As a sophomore in high school, I was a skinny five-foot ten-inches 155 pounds on the baseball field—truly a force to be reckoned with. I knew it would be a long shot for me to make the varsity team with three teammates already committed to play Division I baseball at my position. Months of exercise and discipline later, I made the team as the last guy on the roster. I'll never forget my coach's words:

"Tieds, I'm going to be honest with you, you won't get much playing time, but we're going to keep you because of your work ethic. You motivate the guys."

While riding the pine wouldn't exactly be glorious, it was a victory considering where I started nine months prior to that meeting. Long double practice days starting at 4:45 a.m. and ending around midnight after four AP classes and a two-hour round trip commute through Los Angeles traffic had paid off. I had made the team because I had walked the walk. My example of showing up early to set up the field, paying attention to detail in practice and workouts, and staying late to clean up the field had been noticed. I had proven to everyone that my ego did not matter to me— winning mattered to me.

However, despite this victory, my enthusiasm quickly died off as the season started. I watched my teammates play day after day, knowing I just couldn't match up to their skills. But this isn't how the season ended for me.

In our second game, I got slapped with chart duty. Now if you don't know what chart duty is in baseball, it's probably the sexiest job on the bench next to the foul ball retriever. My job was to watch every pitch and record which kind of pitch each one was and the count in which it was thrown. It's no surprise that baseball players avoid chart duty like the plague.

But eventually, I started to look at my role as more of an opportunity to lead than a mark of inferiority. I realized that even though I was not in a formally understood leadership role, my example was still being followed by those around me. I stopped focusing on climbing the ladder up the depth chart onto the field and began focusing on just exceeding expectations in my role. Not a pitch went by without me charting it and its movement. I took it upon myself to have the discipline and humility to excel in the role I was given, not the one I wish I had, and the results may surprise you.

Eventually, I got so proficient at it, I could pick up patterns in pitch calling by our opponents. By the fifth inning of games, I had a fairly accurate understanding of which pitch was coming before it was called. Furthermore, we would play the same opponents three times in one week, and by our Friday game, I had enough experience to provide useful information to my teammates out on the field. No matter the opponent, inning, or game, my teammates knew I would be on the charts and that I would do everything in my power to help my guys and lead through that job.

I would warm up our outfielders between innings and two of them, both committed to Division I baseball programs, said to me in a game in which we had fallen apart and most of our team had become dejected:

"Not many of the guys are doing their jobs today, but way to do your job in there, keep leading."

This was the proudest moment of that entire season, a season in which I can count on one hand the number of times I batted. I had achieved leadership recognition from two of our best players through leading myself in my supporting, remedial role. Moreover, the other guys on the bench noticed my self-leadership and executed their jobs with the same rigor. Even those without a job found a way to help out, cheering our teammates and working to decipher the opposing team's signs.

By no means did I win any games for us or dramatically influence the outcome of any game. However, I emerged as a leader on the team despite rarely playing because my teammates always knew I was setting the best example I could even though I had a remedial role. Astonishingly, the guy who rarely saw the playing field earned our program's Brian Ulmer award for two years of leadership, high standards, and academic excellence on the varsity team regardless of my role.

Oftentimes, we hear the encouragement to take lemons and make lemonade. But that's too easy. Great leaders find a way to take shitty lemons and make the best lemonade on the market. You know how you become a leader? Take the worst lemons no one wants to work with and make the best product out of them. Show how much you want the team to succeed by taking the toughest jobs no one else wants to do and accomplishing them to the best of your ability for the benefit of the team. People choose to follow those whom they can tell will let nothing stop them from contributing to their team's success.

Obviously, my high school baseball team isn't like working at Goldman Sachs, serving in the military, or playing professional sports. However, the point still stands on any team in any environment that first leading oneself through high standards, discipline, preparation, and enthusiasm is the most effective way to earn your team's trust and buy-in.

One leader who epitomizes the definition of self-leadership is Derek Jeter. Even Red Sox fans will admit that no one exemplified preparation, discipline, and mental toughness the way Jeter did. Perhaps most remarkable about Jeter is that he earned and retained so much respect in a sports market where careers go to be scrutinized—New York City. Jeter himself has described the New York media as "the toughest media environment in sports."[10] Not only is the media demanding, but expectations are always high in a franchise like the Yankees.

So how did Jeter become so successful as the leader of the team? How did this man come to be known simply as "The Captain"? First, he didn't become the leader and then start

10 Derek Jeter, "The Start of Something New," *The Player's Tribune.* October 1 2014.

leading. Jeter focused on being an impeccable self-leader from the day he was drafted in 1996 onward. His teammates followed his leadership because they always knew what to expect with Jeter—exceptional effort 100 percent of the time. When he stepped in the batter's box, everyone in the ballpark knew he had studied film the night before, eaten well that day, arrived early, taken countless ground balls, and focused in batting practice. As my father would say, "You knew his side of the deal was covered."

Although it may sound simple, exuding the confidence that you are prepared and focused is foundational in leadership. If Jimmy wasn't such an exceptional self-leader, he would not have earned his team's trust before they went out into the forest, or when the fog rolled in. Without trust, leadership falls apart because then people resort to what they're programmed to do—save themselves. When people don't trust their leader, they look for ways to avoid blame and responsibility instead of thinking about how to win. No matter what was going on in Major League Baseball, the front office, or the news, Jeter's teammates could always count on him at shortstop to be prepared mentally and physically for every game. For this, they respected him deeply, and respect is the fast track to trust and ultimately cohesive leadership.

When people see someone consistently putting their best foot forward, persevering through pain, and never backing down from challenge, they latch on to that example. They think about that example in times when they want to take a break or let their focus slip. A high performance team in any endeavor has a leader who recognizes how deeply their example resides in the hearts and motivation of their team. It may sound trivial, but leading by example is the simplest way to put it. Words have to match actions in positions of leadership, or else influence and respect are lost. Self-leadership is the art of crafting an ever improving example by which to lead.

Six Steps to Exceptional Self-Leadership

- Identify and embody the example that would motivate you in challenging times.
- Train yourself to maintain mental composure and stay focused in times of strife or crisis.
- Listen to understand rather than to respond.
- Aim for excellence rather than perfection in everything you do.
- Consistently exude passion for your work and life.
- Find something to be grateful for even in the most challenging of circumstances.

CHAPTER 2

VISION

"As a leader, you have to start from the idea that everyone has immeasurable value as an individual."

—PATRICK MCCLENAHAN, CEO OF GOODWILL SOUTHERN CALIFORNIA

"Leadership is the capacity to translate vision into reality."

—WARREN BENNIS

IDENTIFY THE WHY

In June of 2011, Patrick McClenahan watched as 7,500 athletes from 185 countries convened in Athens, Greece, to compete in one of the world's greatest sports spectacles.

Over several weeks, these athletes brought many months of training to bear in twenty-two sports ranging from soccer to gymnastics, hockey, and everything in between. Thousands of spectators were treated to an incredible display of personal commitment and mental fortitude as these athletes pushed through to athletic excellence. After four weeks of competition, inspiration, and memories, these 7,500 athletes had competed their hearts out, going the distance in some of the most challenging Olympic events. The 2011 Games in Athens were a highlight of the power and vitality of the human spirit, but not only for the athletic excellence displayed on the courts, fields, and tracks. The 2011 Games in Athens were not just any Olympic Games. They were the Special Olympics. In those few weeks in Athens, McClenahan's vision for bringing the Special Olympics to his hometown of Los Angeles was born.

McClenahan had many conversations with ordinary people about the Special Olympics and he noticed that many people did not understand the purpose of the Games. He would mention the Games and often hear this response:

"Oh yeah, that's right after the Olympic Games."

And he would say, "No, that's the Paralympic Games."

"Well, what's the difference?"

"The Paralympics games is for athletes with physical disabilities and the Special Olympics is for athletes with mental disabilities."

McClenahan eventually realized that not many people understood the lives of those living with mental disabilities. As members of his family have mental disabilities, this mission, to educate the world on the power of people with mental disabilities became his purpose. McClenahan eventually came up with the vision for changing public perception about people with mental disabilities: educate, inspire, and engage. This was McClenahan's purpose, his why behind his work for four years from 2011 to the closing ceremonies of the 2015 Special Olympics in Los Angeles. His vision propelled him to lead the campaign for the Los Angeles Special Olympics bid and eventually become president and CEO of LA2015 after Los Angeles was awarded the bid.

The most powerful insight behind McClenahan's journey is how his vision to bring the Special Olympics to Los Angeles matched his greater purpose to educate, inspire, and engage people on mental disability. The success of the 2015 Special Olympics was a way to prove his greater purpose to those around him and connect them to the mission as well. McClenahan's vision and purpose behind the Games was clear and consistent from day one to the closing ceremony.

As the Games approached, McClenahan explained that "So much of the Special Olympics is awareness. So many people are uneducated about people with disabilities. What I want most from these games is for people to realize that those with disabilities have value, ability, and importance. These Games change the lives of people around the world who are mistreated and excluded because they are 'different.'"

That steadfast belief in the purpose of changing so many minds about people with mental disabilities through the power of sports resonated with millions of people worldwide. The 2015 Special Olympic Games became a movement with names like Steven Spielberg and President Obama signing on as sponsors and donors. Michelle Obama even flew out to Los Angeles to speak at the opening ceremony in front of sixty-two thousand fans in the Los Angeles Memorial Coliseum.[11] Thousands of volunteers from across Los Angeles flocked to the various venues to take part in the extraordinary event. Nothing summed up the success of the 2015 Special Olympics better than McClenahan's words[12]:

"In a city full of stars, the athletes will be the stars of the show."

---

11 "Michelle Obama and Jamaal Charles join Special Olympics Athletes at 2015 World Games Opening Ceremony," Special Olympics.

12 Kirk Hawkins, "Patrick McClenahan: Embracing the Spirit of Competition," *CSQ*.

McClenahan, a tireless advocate for change around the perception of people with disabilities, would not stop there. His purpose of helping those with disabilities or barriers in life has not waned. He now serves as CEO of Goodwill Southern California. Most understand Goodwill to be a donation center for furniture, clothes, and other items. However, McClenahan again joined for the greater mission of the business: "Transforming Lives Through the Power of Work."

Goodwill Southern California helps remove barriers to employment for people with disabilities and disadvantages including former inmates, military veterans, and dropouts. Using their retail stores and donation centers across Southern California, they fund job training and career counseling services for people. Every year thousands of people enter new jobs and build their lives around their new careers. It's an incredible vision—that people are limitless and have immeasurable value —and one that McClenahan has held his whole life. It's no surprise McClenahan was awarded six Emmy Awards for his documentaries on mental disability and sports and the 2015 Sports Executive of the Year Award for his remarkable work on the 2015 Special Olympics World Games.[13][14]

---

13 Ibid.

14 Special Olympics World Games CEO McClenahan Named Sports Executive of the Year," Fox Sports. January 20 2016.

The many colleagues, athletes, executives, and even US Presidents who have connected to McClenahan and the underlying purpose that has guided his career are a testament to two things:

- His vision's service to other people
- The conviction with which he held that vision

Any leader must have something to which he or she leads their team. If you have a following but no destination, you are a supervisor, not a leader. As young people entering our careers, we need to take the time to discover what truly excites us to lead people as Patrick did so well. The awards and recognition he has received are proof of how he lived to amplify his greater purpose as a leader. If we identify and exemplify our inner, greater purpose as McClenahan did so well, I have no doubt we can achieve the remarkable success he and his teammates achieved.

A common complaint about millennials that I hear from leaders is that we are all always asking the question "Why?" Why do we target these specific clients? Why are we engaging this enemy? Why are we adjusting our business approach in certain regions? Understandably, senior leaders may display some frustration with this trend. No one has the time to constantly explain the methodology and doctrine behind every movement in a corporation.

However, we should not look at the question of "Why?" as a liability and waste of precious time, but rather an investment in what motivates individuals to work as a team. We need to clarify and amplify our why across our teams because people are motivated most by our inner, greater purpose as leaders.

I had an insightful interview with Paul Franklin, a thirty-year veteran of the television business and President of CBS Television Distribution, the network responsible for Judge Judy, Dr. Phil, and Entertainment Tonight. At the tail end of our interview, I asked Paul, "What's the why behind your business?"

"I'm not really sure I understand your question, Hunter," he answered.

"Let me phrase it a different way. Why do you get excited to come to work in the morning? Why do you do this?"

"Well, our job is to make as much money for the network as possible selling our shows. I mean it's a good business."

Clearly, I wasn't getting Paul to understand my point, so I leaned across our table at Uncle Bill's Pancake House and looked him straight in the eye.

I said, "Paul, there's no shame if money is the what. We all have to make a buck and provide for ourselves. But I know money isn't the why. What are you most proud of as a leader at CBS and what do you love about your work?"

Now Paul got it. He said, "Oh, well because it's entertainment! It's fun, I love watching TV and sports."

Indeed, Paul does. Ask him about the NFL Division outlook, the National League pennant race and how his Chicago Cubs are doing, the Lakers' prospects, or his sons playing college baseball, and he's off to the races. Sports and bringing its power to entertain and inspire into family rooms across America is his why. Watching his Chicago Cubs win the World Series in 2016 was probably a great deal sweeter knowing he had helped bring that product that brought him so much joy to more and more families who had been waiting quite a long time for a Cubs title. In short, Paul has a passion for his product and his teammates thrive on that passion.

That wasn't all, though.

He continued, "I love developing people. One of the things I think about most is the people who have worked for me who have gone on to do remarkable things with other networks or started their own networks. I mean I hated like hell to lose them because they were so valuable, but I'm so proud of all they're doing. I can't take credit for their success, but I'm grateful to have played a part in it."

I think Paul gained a deeper understanding of his vision, his why that morning. Every day, he comes to work to satisfy the what, making money for CBS Television selling content and developing strategy for distribution. But beyond that, he comes to work earlier, stays late when he doesn't have to, and goes the extra mile to satisfy his why, to make sure his people are growing and appreciated. His business is his way to fulfill his why, to prove that people have infinite potential within them to grow over the course of a long career and to use sports to entertain families and bring them joy after a long day.

Patrick McClenahan and Paul Franklin may come from two very different sides of the sports world, but they are both guided by an internal, intrinsic vision and purpose behind their work. While McClenahan's purpose is to use sports to prove that people are limitless, Paul's is to use CBS to develop his people into their maximum potential. People connect to these visions as a source of motivation to do their best. This is what drives phenomenal team success: people going beyond the call of duty because they are motivated by an intrinsic purpose shared across their team.

The evidence isn't just anecdotal.

Edward Deci, professor of psychology at the University of Rochester, argued in 1972 that there are two types of motivation—intrinsic and extrinsic. Deci went even further, connecting these two categories of motivation to Maslow's Hierarchy of Needs. Speaking of the ineffectiveness of piece-rate benefits and other employee performance benefits, he argued[15]:

"These rewards can satisfy what Maslow has called "lower order" needs; however, they do not take account of the 'higher order' needs for self-esteem and self-actualization."

He based his paper off of a study in which he asked forty people to complete a puzzle within a time constraint. He varied the experience of the participants into three groups. One group would receive money according to their performance on the puzzle, one group would be threatened with punishment for poor performance, and a third group would be coached along by the experimenters. After time was up, each group was given a cool-down period of eight minutes. Not surprisingly, the people who were coached with feedback spent significantly more of their free eight minutes working on the remainder of the puzzle than did those in the groups who were motivated by money or fear.

---

15 Edward, Deci. "The Effect of Contingent and Noncontingent Rewards and Controls on Intrinsic Motivation." *Organizational Behavior and Human Performance* 8 (1972): 218.

This was a landmark study that demonstrated the power of intrinsic motivation. In other words, these people desired more than a paycheck at the end of the day. The key now is for leaders to practice connecting their teams to intrinsic sources of motivation: their why and purpose. Deci summed it up well in his study that money cannot produce sustained intrinsic motivation[16]:

"While extrinsic rewards like money can certainly motivate behavior, they appear to be doing so at the expense of intrinsic motivation."

All of this is just a scientific way of saying something we already know to be true. If you want people to do their best for your team, you have to give them a why that creates intrinsic motivation. People who are motivated extrinsically will need ever more extrinsic rewards to maintain their current level of output. As a leader, it would be a mistake to think answering the question of "Why?" is a waste of time. In fact, it's one of the most valuable assets you have as a leader. The most effective leaders became so by first refining their why so that people would feel intrinsically motivated to jump on the train.

What's your why? What motivates you to lead people and bring them toward your goal? In a world where it's so easy

---

16 Ibid, 224.

to do the bare minimum, what is it that drives you to do more and be more for your teammates? For McClenahan, it was the need to educate, inspire, and engage people about mental disability. For me, it's to create and coach awesome leaders. Invest in determining the cause and purpose that motivates you to lead with a great example. Leading by example becomes much easier when your mission matches your inner purpose.

Notice how McClenahan's purpose, his why, focused on serving other people. Whatever you determine your why to be, I promise you can fulfill it better by connecting it to others. Find a purpose that builds other people and you will find yourself more motivated than ever when challenges come your way. It's easy to give up in times of trial when you are at the center of your why. But, when other people are your why, you won't let them down that easily.

When people are your purpose, not only will you not let them down easily, but they won't let you down either. People who know their leader's purpose above all else is serving them will push even further for that leader. A recent study of pre-medical college students discovered an important connection between student-oriented professors and their students' intrinsic motivation.[17] In other words, the more

17 Cesar Orzini, Phillip Evans, and Oscar Jerez. "How to Encourage Intrinsic Motivation in the Clinical Teaching Environment?

these students felt their professor focused on their success and satisfying their academic needs, the more intrinsically motivated these students were to perform in these exceedingly difficult classes. This is extremely powerful because these students were not working harder because they suddenly desired better grades, a sign of extrinsic motivation. Rather, they improved preparation and performance because they felt intrinsically motivated by the pursuit of excellence and not letting their professor down. When your teammates know that they are an integral part of your inner purpose, they turn that care into performance.

COMMUNICATE THE WHY WITH CONVICTION

On June 12th, 1987 President Ronald Reagan spoke the most famous six words of his presidency, a sentence that would prove to be one of the defining moments in the Cold War. On a brisk morning in front of the Brandenburg Gate in Berlin, President Reagan spoke before a crowd of thousands of West Berlin citizens[18]:

"Mr. Gorbachev, tear down this wall."

A Systematic Review from the Self-Determination Theory." *Journal of Educational Evaluation for Health Professionals* vol. 12, no. 8 (2015)

18 "Berlin Wall," The Ronald Reagan Presidential Library and Museum.

The crowd roared with a fervor that yearned for freedom. Sound turned into feeling as thousands cheered President Reagan's call to free East Berlin.

Although it was a quintessential moment of Reagan's Presidency, the 1980s, and even the twentieth century, it almost never happened. Numerous officials in the Reagan Administration from Deputy Secretary of Defense Colin Powell to White House Chief of Staff Howard Baker argued that the speech sounded "extreme" and "unpresidential."[19] Many officials were worried about the line sparking further geopolitical tensions with Mikhail Gorbachev, with whom Reagan had invested much time and energy to build a working relationship[20]. In the days leading up to Reagan's speech, the line was debated vocally and forcefully, being removed and added back in multiple times. Reagan's advisors could not come to any sort of consensus on the line.

But it didn't matter.

Reagan was going to say it the entire time. It was his conviction to proclaim the moral repulsiveness of the Berlin

---

19 Kenneth Walsh, "Seizing the Moment: Memorable Presidential Speeches are Few and Far Between. But Ronald Reagan's Words in Berlin Two Decades Ago Will Live On." US News and World Report.

20 Peter Robinson, "'Tear Down This Wall': How Top Advisors Opposed Reagan's Challenge to Gorbachev-But Lost." *National Archives Prologue Magazine* Vol. 39, No. 2 (Summer 2007).

Wall. In fact, it was Reagan's original conviction that the citizens of Germany and the world needed to hear that this wall was morally wrong, regardless of political consequences. As Anthony Dolan, chief speechwriter of the Reagan Administration explained, he had a meeting with President Reagan in advance of the trip to Berlin before the speechwriting department ever conceived of the speech. Dolan asked the President:

"Mr. President, it's still very early, but we were just wondering if you had any thoughts at all yet on the Berlin speech?"

President Reagan knew that he wanted Germany and the world to hear before anyone put any ideas or objections in his mind. He raised his hand, dropped it on the desk and responded[21]:

"Well, tear down the wall."

Reagan's conviction was that the world needed to know from American leadership that the Berlin Wall was morally bankrupt and evil. Whenever Reagan spoke about international affairs, he spoke with incredibly forceful conviction about the urgency of securing freedom to as many people as possible. Reagan spoke with a confidence that his side, freedom, had

---

21 Anthony Dolan, "Four Little Words," The Wall Street Journal.

to prevail no matter the costs. Reagan knew his purpose and he would not be deterred from living that purpose as a leader. The State Department and National Security Council submitted alternate drafts of the speech all the way up until the day of the speech. But Reagan held firm in his conviction and purpose, telling Deputy Chief of Staff Kenneth Duberstein on the limousine ride to the Brandenburg Gate[22]:

"The boys at State are going to kill me, but it's the right thing to do."

When you communicate your vision to your people, do you make clear just how much you believe in that vision and the power of the why behind that vision? Whenever Reagan gave a speech, he made sure that not only would viewers understand the message he was communicating, but also that they would feel the emotion and confidence with which he delivered his message, that oppressed people deserved freedom. If a leader doesn't deliver their vision with conviction, it reflects lack of preparation and confidence on the part of the leader and no one chooses to follow those leaders. Communicate your vision not just to inform, but to touch and inspire to action.

22 Peter Robinson, "'Tear Down This Wall': How Top Advisors Opposed Reagan's Challenge to Gorbachev-But Lost." *National Archives Prologue Magazine* Vol. 39, No. 2 (Summer 2007).

LET THEM OWN THE WHY

5:50 a.m. groggy and half asleep, I stepped out of the car into the brisk Los Angeles early morning darkness. It was October 1, signaling the beginning of the high school baseball season in Southern California where baseball is a culture more than an activity. From now until graduation day in early June of next year, my Loyola teammates and I would be training to win a Mission League Title and California Interscholastic Federation (CIF) Division I Championship. October would be the only relatively easy month when we only trained four days a week, picking up to six days per week in November all the way through the season. Add in the glorious Los Angeles traffic commuting twenty miles each way plus Loyola High School's rigorous college preparatory AP coursework and you have one hell of an eight-month grind.

Anyway, this was day one, but not just any day one. Many of our friends who played football and basketball had already begun training and told us stories all through September about the new strength and conditioning coach, Andre Woodert. An outstanding USC Trojan running back, brilliant student, and masterof kinesiology and fitness, Coach Woodert embodied excellence in every area of his life. He was well-built, well-read, and well-respected—a true self-leader.

That doesn't mean we were not absolutely terrified of him though. Our football and basketball teammates told us stories of their teams throwing up and nearly quitting during workouts. Throughout September, we watched guys come out of the weight room before school drenched in sweat, looking as if they had just endured Boot Camp. Worst of all, we watched guys come into class late due to the dreaded "intensity circle." If members of the team were not putting out and pushing themselves hard enough in the weight room, the entire team faced the intensity circle.

If a sports team received an intensity circle, they had to drop all weights and equipment and sprint across campus to the football field in thirty seconds, gathering around the Loyola "L" at midfield to learn the importance of discipline, teamwork, and leadership. The workout in the gym would be made up another time. For now, these poor souls had another thing coming.

We would hear rumors at lunch and in class: "Did you hear, the soccer team had an intensity circle this morning..."

The team faced a barrage of tasks and calisthenics designed to rebuild the universal commitment to the team expected of each individual that had been lacking in the weight room. Burpees, pushups, and sit ups had to be finished in perfect unison as a team before reentering the weight room and these sessions extended for quite some time. The absolute last thing you wanted in an Andre workout was to receive an intensity circle because you were about to have your ass handed to you and chances are you would be late to class. And the second to last thing you wanted was to have to walk into a Jesuit's class late during the morning prayer.

With all of these warnings in mind, we gathered our bearings and made sure we were ready at 6:00 a.m. sharp in the weight room. An aura of uncertainty surrounded the group, anxious about how we would hold up under this notoriously difficult workout regimen. Not a second after 6:00 a.m., Coach Woodert entered and he immediately laid the floor plan for our training over the next few months. Needless to say, he knew his shit.

"Teenage baseball players are weak in many areas that can cause long-term injury prospects. Pitchers must build leg and core strength to generate more power and alleviate wear on elbows and shoulders. Position players need to build leg and forearm strength to withstand the strain of swinging and throwing continuously. This will be a difficult process and it's vitally important that you take care of yourselves."

We all nodded, trying not to think about what this would involve.

"Teenage athletes consume resources faster than anyone else because you are constantly growing. Chances are that each one of you is dehydrated right now. Every workout I expect you all to have a gallon of water with you and finish it throughout the day to keep your system fueled properly. Additionally, you all need to have two lacrosse balls to massage sore muscles and rebuild after workouts."

It was a thoroughly methodical process. Coach Woodert had obviously invested much time and effort into us, as individuals and as a team. He wanted us to get stronger so we could stay healthy. He wanted us to drink water and use foam rollers so we could recuperate and get the most out of the effort we put in with him in the weight room. He saw us as long-term athletes who could play in college and perhaps even beyond. He inspired that confidence and work-horse mentality with the way he carried himself. Not only did he want us to get stronger physically, he wanted us to fortify our minds as individuals and as teammates so that we could achieve our best together.

"I'm sure you guys have heard about me. I expect a lot out of you guys. Every time we enter this weight room, I expect you all to give me every last ounce of effort you have for your own benefit and the benefit of the team. If one member of the team isn't giving everything he has, the team as a whole is suffering. With that said, I am going to introduce you all to something we call... the intensity circle."

"What? What did we do? It's been five minutes. How could we have screwed up already?" I thought to myself as I said my prayers on the way to the field.

Most people think Los Angeles is always warm and sunny, but the reality is that it's a desert and it's cold before the sun rises. When it's windy in the mid-forties and you're wearing shorts and a thin workout shirt, the cold and the expectation of an ass kicking just pierce you.

"Time is scarce and we need the utmost intensity every day we work out together. If we start losing intensity, this is how we will get it back. Circle up."

We circled up around the center of the field and then his football background emerged.

"Chatter your feet in place."

Immediately, we chattered our feet like our lives depended on it.

"When I say 'down,' everyone needs to drop into a pushup position. However, I am not going to say 'up.' That's your job. You will all come up together as one unit and repeat the number we just did together. If we lose count or we lose team coordination, we will start over and we need one hundred to get back to the weight room. If you guys can do this together at 6 a.m. in the cold, you can definitely turn a double play in the bottom of the seventh inning in May."

The situation looked like a scene straight out of *Remember the Titans*. Needless to say, none of us were prepared for this challenge and we started over many times. Somehow we made it back to the weight room that day, but the lesson was crystal clear: expectations have been set and communicated, and they must be met as a team because the team deserves the best from each individual.

Although I was initially terrified by what was to come that season and awestruck by Coach Woodert's knowledge, as time passed I realized the power behind his tactics. He was sharing his knowledge with us not because he wanted to show off, but because he wanted us to understand at a fundamental level why we needed to follow him. Every day he gave us a value proposition, a reason to buy into his leadership that would benefit us as a team—strengthening ourselves and improving teamwork.

We knew it would be incredibly challenging and expectations would be set high, but we did not mind because he had earned our followership by giving us the why behind our investment. He was explaining to us the greater purpose behind every challenge and exercise he threw at us because he knew that greater purpose would motivate us more than anything else. Most importantly, that purpose was focused on us and helping us excel.

He wouldn't tell us to push through the workouts so we could rest and escape the pain. He would push us to finish on time with perfect technique every time because he wanted us to be protected from injury. He wouldn't tell us to hold a team plank longer than the soccer team for the satisfaction. Rather, he did this to push us to get comfortable relying on one another in stressful situations. With time, we began to do this ourselves, understanding the purpose behind each day and turning each day into an investment in our future selves. We began to own the why because Coach Woodert made the why about us!

Coach Woodert is a phenomenal leader because he set expectations and created high team expectations through his self-leadership, motivating us to meet those expectations with an intrinsic purpose that focused on us. Whenever he entered the weight room, instantly a culture of excellence, urgency, and commitment rushed in with him that spread through us like wildfire. When he explained a new technique, he showed us why he wanted it done this way and most importantly how it would benefit us in the season. We trusted his methodology because he lived it through his credibility. Excellent leaders use their self-leadership and standards to not only set expectations, but inspire the confidence in a team to meet those expectations, not letting them lose their commitment or urgency. Never forget how powerful your example and purpose are to your team's mission because your teammates are always watching and feeding off of you.

One of the responses I get about this story and lesson is that it's just too difficult or expensive to communicate a greater purpose effectively to all of your people. There is certainly credence to this argument, but I would encourage you to think about it in terms of an investment. Communicating your vision to your people is an investment, otherwise they are left guessing what their greater purpose is at work. Also, what are you losing in terms of enthusiasm and productivity by not energizing people about your mission? Patrick McClenahan will be the first one to tell you that Goodwill Southern California attributes its success to spreading the same purpose across every sector of their business. The cashiers working the retail stores and the community engagement teams helping people find jobs both have the same greater purpose: transforming lives through the power of work. The great your purpose, the greater your motivation and success.

If you're still skeptical, let me tell you about how letting people own their why has proven wildly successful and has actually changed the world.

Senator Barack Obama catapulted to national prominence on November 4th, 2008 when he defeated Senator John McCain in the US Presidential Election, becoming the United States' first African-American president. In just five years, Obama went from an Illinois State Senator to US Senator to the Democratic Party's Presidential Nominee and eventually forty-fourth President of the United States. However, he faced a major issue in his 2012 reelection campaign. He needed the usual Democratic voter turnout and then some to win. It became clear that one voter group in particular, young voters ages eighteen to twenty-nine, would make the difference. As Van Jones said on CNN before the election, "If the youth vote shrinks, Obama's toast."[23] The only problem was that this age group notoriously fails to turn out.

Enter Lenny Stern, an advertising guru who specializes in political campaigns, and co-owner of SS&K advertising. It would be safe to say that SS&K's advertisements targeting young voters turned them out for Obama and pushed him over the edge to electoral victory. I interviewed Mr. Stern because I was so interested in how he started this movement among young voters to get involved in 2012 election and re-elect President Obama.

His answer was simple: "Connect to their why first, then introduce President Obama and his why."

---

23 "Obama vs. Romney: Election Eve Rallies," CNN Election Center. November 5 2012.

I was shocked, "It cannot be that simple though. Millions of young voters registered and turned out. There's no way it was just a congruence of their whys?"

"Yes, it is. We made them owners of their own movement. We made the campaign about them and used their own language to connect with them on their turf."

It was out of this strategy that the I Pledge Campaign was born. SS&K took the Pledge of Allegiance and met young voters where they were on the issues they cared about. Tens of thousands of young voters wrote their reason for voting Obama, their pledge, on their hand and shared it on social media. Each individual felt that they owned a piece of the Obama platform, a piece of his greater purpose.

President Obama embodied hope and change for the nation at every step of the campaign—that was his why. Millennials are the generation that lives and breathes all things change. What Lenny and his team recognized was that millennials would be far more motivated to jump on President Obama's campaign, donate, and vote if they owned the movement, meaning that they felt a certain deep connection to the greater purpose of the campaign: change. And that was how many millennials felt, that they owned this movement to elect a change-oriented president.

The results were astounding as millennial voters turned out in droves. 1.25 million more young voters voted for Obama in 2012 than in 2008, helping President Obama win key swing states like Kentucky, Pennsylvania, Florida, and Ohio.[24] The reason behind this incredible movement? The leaders let the followers own the why behind their movement.

I was immensely surprised, but there is a simple formula for employing an effective vision as a leader:

- Articulate a vision with a societal goal
- Communicate that vision with conviction
- Let your teammates own the vision

If you do those three things with regard to your vision as a leader, you will undoubtedly create a more effective, energized team. Not only will your team achieve higher performance, but they will also be excited to carry out the vision even more when challenging times arise. Thousands donated to the Los Angeles Special Olympics, 1.25 million more millennials voted for Obama, and my baseball team excelled because leadership articulated a vision with conviction and let us own that vision.

24 "Obama 2012," SS&K Advertising.

CHAPTER 3

CULTURE

"Culture isn't the most important thing. It's the only thing."

—JIM SINEGAL COFOUNDER AND FORMER CEO OF COSTCO

"Bad protocol and processes beat good people every time."

—FIRST LIEUTENANT PETER COHEN, USMC

"Culture is the collective personality of an organization."

—JEFF WEINER CEO OF LINKEDIN

While self-leadership and vision are foundational, they are powerless without an engine: people and culture. One of the questions I received most during the course of this project is "Why does culture even matter?" My own dad, an excellent self-leader, teammate, and motivator, even added, "Well, what's the difference between culture and expectations? Just set clear expectations and you won't have a problem."

Although my dad is usually right on many subjects, I pushed back on him here. Culture is so integral to leadership because it lays the groundwork for all you do as a leader. Culture is the gatekeeper to your success as a leader. You can go through all the effort of molding yourself into the strongest self-leader and crafting a practical, yet innovative vision, but those assets only take root in your team if placed within the proper culture. Otherwise, you will see all of your effort repelled like a magnet.

Leaders have the same twenty-four hours a day as the rest of us and many even employ assistants to help them manage their time and schedule. To add "Establishing culture of effort, execution, and enthusiasm" to the already headache-inducing to-do list is probably one of the last things you feel like doing as a leader. However, establishing culture early is integral to your success because it provides a blueprint for growth and complements the leader's example. If you don't believe me, take a look at LinkedIn.

Jeff Weiner has accomplished some remarkable feats in his nine-year tenure as CEO of LinkedIn. The company has added new networking products and begun fighting unemployment in cities with historically high unemployment rates using their job and skills data. It's no surprise LinkedIn's employees named Weiner one of Glassdoor's "Top Ten CEOs at U.S. Tech Companies."[25] The company now has nearly twelve thousand employees and offices around the world. Do you know when Weiner established and refined the company's culture around "integrity, collaboration, humor, results, and transformation?" Back when they had just 340 employees.[26] LinkedIn, one of the most successful companies of the last twenty years, focused on culture first. Culture creates success, success does not create culture.

The bottom line is this: as a leader, if you don't set the culture, someone else will. Furthermore, there's no guarantee that your self-leadership style and vision fit into that culture. And once cultures are established, they are extremely difficult to change and improve.

To be clear, although we have demonstrated the importance of establishing your culture early on around your self-leadership and vision for success, the culture is for everyone not just you. Your teammates still have to buy into your culture,

---

25 Dennis McCafferty, "The Top 10 CEOs at US Tech Companies," Baseline, April 8 2014.

26 Jeff Weiner, "Jeff Weiner on Establishing a Culture and a Plan for Scaling," Lynda.com. January 17 2017.

self-leadership, and vision, meaning you still have to earn it from them. The best way to do this is to include them in the process. Not only does this show them visibly that you care about the experience they have at work, but it also gives them a sense of ownership over the way their company operates and presents itself to clients and outside stakeholders. If you're ever in doubt about this, as yourself, "Would I be more or less motivated to come to work if my boss asked me my opinion on our culture, values, and expectations?" Let that answer guide how you include your teammates.

Now that we've established that culture matters and that we must define it early in our leadership tenure, what exactly constitutes effective culture? There can certainly be no once-size-fits-all approach to organizational culture. The Marines may need a culture slightly different from my high school baseball team. However, I have settled on three main focal points of an effective culture that elevates your teammates.

I call it the Three E's of effective culture: Effort, Execution, and Enthusiasm. No matter your industry or organization, I promise these three tenets will improve your culture and performance because they all ask you and your teammates to control things within your jurisdiction as individuals. We cannot control so many of the factors in our lives that cause stress and diminish performance. However, we can mitigate the effects of factors beyond our control by establishing our culture around three powerful factors which we can control: effort, execution, and enthusiasm.

EFFORT

At the close of the Major League Baseball regular season in 1987, the Los Angeles Dodgers seemed completely out of the picture as playoff contenders the next season. Finishing sixteen games below five hundred and well out of the National League West race, the Dodgers knew they needed to make some dramatic personnel moves that offseason. Although they faced a monumental challenge in returning the Dodgers to their competitive standard in the National League, they took an approach many at the time did not understand, but has since become exceedingly clear among businesses and organizations around the world—hiring to culture.

Several moves stunned the Dodger fan base, especially dealing away reliable pitcher Bob Welch. However, their next move would prove to be among their most monumental, shifting their culture from the laid back West Coast ball club to a serious, competitive team ready to stare down any opponent. On January 29, 1988, the Dodgers signed free agent Kirk Gibson from the Detroit Tigers and the culture improvement officially began.

Gibson was a six-foot-four 230-pound former linebacker from Michigan State University. Although a football player by training, he chose baseball over football for his long-term health, eventually becoming a star on the Detroit Tigers. He brought a football mentality to the baseball field and immediately earned leadership responsibility with his reputation as an intense and gritty competitor.

You knew before he even walked in the dugout that he was ready to compete because he was a self-leader. On top of that, he had the necessary vision—to win the World Series and restore the Dodgers to prominence. He had the tangibles and intangibles we have already discussed as integral to leadership, and as you will see, those foundational aspects led to his successful implementation of a new winning culture in Los Angeles.

On the first day of spring training, Gibson reported bright and early to the field in Peoria, Arizona. He was among the first onto the field, stretching, throwing, running sprints, and working up a sweat. However, his new teammates decided to have a little fun with their new teammate and smeared eye black all over the inside of Gibson's cap. When Gibson went to wipe the sweat off of his forehead, he smeared all of the sticky black sunscreen around his face. Although initially dumbfounded, Gibson eventually realized the practical joke that had been pulled on him[27].

He stormed off the field, furious at what had happened, yelling, "No wonder this team finished in last place!"

Dodger manager Tommy Lasorda wondered what had happened and followed Gibson into the locker room. The media thought Gibson had hurt himself and wondered all day what was wrong. To avoid bad press, the Dodgers asked Gibson to say he had just come down with some illness that day, rather than say he had left practice because of teammates fooling around.

But Kirk Gibson refused. He wouldn't lie about the culture in the Dodger clubhouse to save face for the organization. He knew they would have a losing season again if the professional, competitive culture they promoted to the outside world did not match the culture within the locker room. He told the media how his team had pulled a stupid prank on him on the first day of spring training and he was sure upset about it.

"He was just trying to have some fun with you, Gibson" one teammate tried to contend.

---

27 "Only in Hollywood," Sportsnet LA. July 15 2018.

Gibson's only response was, "You think this is fun? Going sixteen games under five hundred isn't fun. Winning is fun!"[28]

Clearly, there was a new sheriff in town. Gibson's culture of bringing a hard-nosed, competitive, effort-driven culture to the Dodgers ignited a season that would go down in history. Orel Hershiser broke Don Drysdale's record for the longest streak of scoreless innings and the Dodgers would go on to win the World Series as underdogs against the Oakland Athletics. Nothing epitomized the Dodgers' new culture of toughness and competitiveness like Kirk Gibson's timeless walk-off homerun in the Game 1 of the World Series after sustaining injuries to both legs in the previous series. [29]

If people are the lifeblood of your organization, culture is your immune system. Culture addresses the largest problems you will face in your business or unit before those problems enter the door, such as apathy and lack of attention to detail. When these principles— maximum effort and attention to detail— are baked into a culture that reflects your self-leadership and vision as a leader, they become your best allies in creating an effective team. In a culture of maximum effort, people go above and beyond not because they fear consequences, but because they feel an obligation to themselves,

---

28 Ibid.

29 Ibid.

their potential, and their teammates to do their best at all times. In other words, culture creates more intrinsic motivation while fear of consequences produces more extrinsic motivation.

We hear how important culture is from countless executives, coaches, and leaders. But how often do we actually block out time in the week to think about how our culture is affecting performance? Many people understand that culture is important, but we don't invest the time to seriously pinpoint an effective culture. When was the last time you sat down in a culture meeting? I'm guessing a long time ago, if at all. As a leader, take inventory of how your example is interpreted and followed from an effort standpoint. The apple does not fall from the tree. Chances are that if you notice your teammates giving less than their best effort, it started with their leader breaking the culture and creating an example of inadequate effort.

ENTHUSIASM

Aaron Teats is the Chief Marketing Officer of the Anaheim Ducks hockey club, responsible for every aspect of marketing of the entire club from ticket sales to community service in Anaheim, California. It's a monumental task for a team to accomplish, yet they do a remarkable job despite the challenges of the industry. When people go to professional sporting events, many overlook the difficulty of the schedules and lives of those who work for the teams. Sports are entertainment, a way to enjoy your time away from work. But when your work is marketing sports and promoting your team, your busy times and deadlines fall on your weekends and evenings, when everyone else wants to be entertained. Add in the normal nine to five on weekdays and you have a challenging work schedule for the marketing team at the Anaheim Ducks. The work is demanding and time sensitive as there are only so many games and community events throughout the season.

However, despite all these challenges, the Anaheim Ducks continue to be among the most successful, philanthropic franchises in the National Hockey League, posting incredible playoff runs, impressive ticket sales, and a consistent standing as one of the most philanthropic teams.

So how do Aaron and his team accomplish all this success? I hesitate to say it's just one great leader and Aaron would be the first to tell you his staff is the most dedicated, teamwork-driven group out there. But Aaron uses some great leadership techniques to achieve these goals that I think will benefit you whenever your organization faces tight deadlines, demanding schedules, and challenging tasks. He uses the Anaheim Ducks' culture of enthusiasm to guard against this influence on his team.

From the very first moment new hires walk in the door, Aaron focuses on imparting the Ducks' culture:

"By the time a new hire gets to me, you've already demonstrated you know how to do the job. I'm not worried about that. I'm here to help you understand why you're being hired. You are here to help facilitate a culture. Period."

I have to say, I looked back at Aaron in disbelief. His team is remarkably successful so how could his approach be so simple? I drove two hours through Los Angeles traffic down to the Honda Center where the Ducks play, thinking he was going to reveal his secret weapons like advanced data analytics and demographic research on their fan base. I'm sure Aaron is well-versed on those topics as well, but he did not mention those as his primary assets. Instead, his primary asset as the leader of this incredibly successful marketing team is a culture centered on enthusiasm in the face of challenges, deadlines, and stressful conditions. Why did Aaron make it abundantly clear to me that his team's culture matters more than their regression analyses? He made that point because he understands that culture creates a collective attitude that permeates the organization. It's almost as if each member of the team has "Duck" as their middle name because they are all united by this culture orientation from Aaron.

"I am trusting that you will teach us a lot from your schooling. But what they don't teach you in school is culture. You are assuming great responsibility as a new member of this team that we have a positive, enthusiastic attitude in our culture."

Aaron could talk about anything in his first meeting with new hires. Yet, what does he drill into new team members? He teaches them that their culture of enthusiasm is their primary weapon and uniting force as a team and it should be for your team too. Not only does this culture enhance the team morale, but it also maintains that high team morale when the going gets tough in the office. When the chips are down in the season and deadlines are approaching, handling these situations with poise, skill, and enthusiasm is second nature because they all received the same culture orientation about how enthusiasm will drive success regardless of circumstances.

"You're going to have really tough days. We all do—where the work comes down on you and you make mistakes, work for a long time, and get frustrated. But if we can do everything to maintain a positive culture, we are taking a step forward in handling those challenging times effectively."

Culture generates an attitude and your attitude is just as effective as your skills and training in generating success. As opposed to external factors such as the market, the economy, higher management, or difficult clients, we can control our attitude through our culture. Aaron recognized this early in his leadership career and it has paid off handsomely in how well the Ducks have progressed and how well his teammates handle hardship that stems from beyond their control.

This is not to say that a cultural orientation is enough to establish a lasting, effective culture. The whole point of a culture is that it is reinforced consistently and forcefully through a common connection among team members. Think of any sociological or religious culture. Christmas, Yom Kippur, Ramadan, July 4th, and Cinco de Mayo are all annual events that unite members of a culture back to a significant event. As a leader, do your best to think of ways you can create events or anniversaries like these that unite all members of your team regardless of role. Perhaps an annual retreat, dinner, or extracurricular, intramural event in which you focus on what runs parallel throughout your entire team— collective purpose and culture.

In addition to creating a positive attitude in your organization, a culture of enthusiasm repels one of the most destructive forces in a difficult situation—the feeling of victimhood. Exceptional leaders do not let their people fall into the trap of feeling like victims in trying situations. Remember from Chapter 1 on self-leadership, the primary job of the leader is to communicate the vision and internal motivation for their team's goal.

Victimhood leads to diminished internal motivation and the feeling of helplessness. No one wants to push through hardship, grind, and fight to win when they feel as though circumstance controls them and some outside force is lobbying for their demise. This is definitely not to say that people fall victim to the trials of life. There is certainly an immense amount of suffering out there. However, the point stands that leaders motivate their teams with their attitude in these difficult situations, repelling the deflating influence of victimhood.

How do effective leaders do this? Self-leadership and reliance on culture and processes. I want us to think about football teams running the two-minute drill, where the team on offense is losing by one score with two minutes on the clock to get into the endzone. Furthermore, think of the situation when a missed call, penalty, or dropped pass puts the team in third down and long. This is a time when victimhood can settle in because the pressure is on, the challenge is at hand, and most destructively, there are ample excuses to be made. But what do successful teams and leaders do on the field in this situation?

The leader—oftentimes the quarterback, running back, or center—starts by leading themselves as an individual. They exhibit the poise and neglect of excuses that is expected of the rest of the team. In other words, they hold their emotions in check while demonstrating the desired behavior. Next, they rely on culture to create an attitude of resilience. If done properly, these leaders have been reinforcing this example in practice, just as Aaron did in the offseason with the Ducks. Finally, they rely on processes, picking up play calls, communicating, adjusting formations, and performing the fundamentals correctly.

Processes set in place for the two-minute drill provide a clear route for progress and coordination in the face of difficult odds, limited resources, and the corrupting influence of victimhood peering over your shoulder. What pushes people beyond victimhood is someone else rising above it. It's imperative that you are prepared to make that decision to rise above it as the leader.

EXECUTION

When building your team, it is important to understand that you are building a task force. Building your team is analogous to walking through Home Depot picking up the tools you will need for the job. Picking the right people does not ensure that you will not encounter problems in the organization you lead, but it does ensure that you will face manageable problems as opposed to problems of character and ethics. As Jeff Weiner explained to us, it's important to set the culture early and then hire and scale around that culture, building a team around your culture not the other way around.

For Gregg Throgmartin, President of Fabletics and former Chief Operating Officer of HH Gregg, a major Midwest appliances retail chain, culture is defined by execution. We don't mean the old fashioned, execute or hit the road, move up or move out approach. After all, if success would just follow from a command, we wouldn't need to study organizational behavior and leadership. But what Gregg preaches and I stand by is the importance of emphasizing aggressiveness as a facet of culture. What follows from emphasizing aggressiveness and execution is people begin to value learning and growth more than perfection. Oftentimes, what prevents us from executing our plan as individuals is the fear of mistakes, poor timing, or harming our reputation. Gregg has a unique method for creating a culture around execution that just may surprise you.

I asked him, "Gregg, how did you create a culture of execution that propelled HH Gregg all those years?"

I could have never predicted his response. He replied, "It all started with our hiring. It's far easier to hire motivated people who want to execute, whom we can develop, than it is to hire highly-skilled, yet unmotivated people whom we have to push to execute the playbook."

I was intrigued by his answer, but I didn't think it could be this simple—just hire motivated people who want to execute.

Gregg continued, "The majority of our vice presidents and managers actually come from the fast food and construction industries. When we hired new managers, we recruited Hardee's managers and construction workers. These people had been working at a Hardee's until 2 a.m. and managing the lunch rush. We knew they understood the importance of execution and we wanted them to enhance that culture."

I couldn't believe what was being confirmed right before my eyes. The formula for success really is quite simple—hire motivated people who want to execute and give them the right playbook and tools to succeed. In other words, hire to culture. Most importantly, when you create a culture of execution around your team, your job as a leader and manager becomes much easier. Your main focus shifts from ensuring the team stays on task to removing barriers to their execution of the plan. Imagine you're a leader on a ship. What sounds easier and more effective as a leader—spending time in the engine room managing the engine or in the wheelhouse navigating toward the goal? A culture of execution allows leaders to worry less about the team's day-to-day conduct and focus more on the long-term course of the organization. In other words, a culture of execution promotes teamwork between the operations and strategy arms of an organization. The strategy side enjoys the confidence that its operations team will execute the plan forcefully, and the operations side trusts that the strategy team has examined all options for the best route.

I realized the immense managerial advantage behind Gregg's approach as I debriefed our interview. With a culture of execution, the problems you face usually come down to communication, rather than lack of effort or conviction in executing the plan. Lapses or misunderstandings in communication are much easier to address from a leadership standpoint than character-level deficiencies in motivation, attention to detail, and willingness to execute. This makes decision-making much easier because you have greater confidence that the plan will be executed well. Your teammates still have to believe in the mission to execute it, but it allows you the greater freedom to focus on communicating that vision effectively as a leader. And as Gregg taught me, communication usually proves to be the Achilles heel of a team.

Gregg explained, "Normally what causes poor performance on a team is ineffective communication from the leader. No one genuinely wants to underperform or disappoint, but you have to diagnose why. As the leader, when you're wrong, you have to own the error and take the blame for not communicating well enough."

None of these insights attempt to argue that culture and emphasis on execution can prevent mistakes. Mistakes will always be a problem of any and every organization. Organizations and teams are just groups of people, and it's a certainty that people will make mistakes. However, a culture of execution allows those mistakes to be of a manageable variety and eventually be turned into assets. Gregg is the first one to tell you that he rarely ever dealt with apathy, lack of integrity or grit in HH Gregg's vice presidents and managers. When mistakes happen, his employees were hungry to get back in the game and use those mistakes to improve themselves as managers and employees because it's a facet of their company culture.

In addition to synchronizing strategy and operations and mitigating serious mistakes, a culture of execution creates an environment where people are empowered by their work, regardless of their role in the organizational hierarchy. A culture of execution binds all stakeholders by showing that everyone has the same devotion to the organization regardless of rank. It lets everyone in the organization know from entry level to board room that people come here to this office, branch, or unit to contribute and execute their role as a team player. Some roles may include more responsibility, attention, and recognition than others, but executing the plan and mission of the organization is clearly made paramount to role. Furthermore, we create an environment where people know excelling in their role is rewarded.

I asked Gregg about this topic when hiring these new managers: "So what was that like in hiring meetings when you wanted to recruit these managers from Hardee's and construction? Was there much pushback?"

Immediately, Gregg responded, "Definitely. I mean the world would say these people were C's, but we saw A's in them. We cannot teach enthusiasm and grit, but we can teach the skillsets required to operate the warehouse, manage stores, and oversee the logistics and sales operations."

I was profoundly moved by this aspect of HH Gregg's culture because their culture of execution is just an expression of Gregg Throgmartin's greater purpose. Gregg's core belief is that where someone comes from is insignificant in relation to where they are going. He values one's commitment to execution and dedication more than their background. He sees no reason why anyone who is committed cannot excel at his company. This culture is just a way for Gregg to prove what he believes about the world: that anyone with drive can create their success. HH Gregg's culture of execution provides the avenue for his people to prove that principle to be true at work every day. I promise that if you make your culture an expression of your belief in peoples' talents and dedication, you will experience phenomenal growth in your organization just as Gregg did with his team.

In summary, culture fosters an attitude in your organization. Kirk Gibson, Aaron Teats, and Gregg Throgmartin all used culture to drive their success by establishing effort, enthusiasm, and execution in their teams' respective cultures. They were successful in creating these effective cultures because they lived them as individuals. The best way to create the culture you desire is to embody the culture you desire. Making a conscious effort to create events and reminders of your culture will convey to your teammates that you treat culture as an asset, not a footnote. Think of the kind of attitude you want your team to display in the bottom of the ninth inning when the chips are down, and focus your efforts on creating that culture. As always, your self-leadership and mission will drive the success of this endeavor. As retired Marine Corps General and Secretary of Defense James Mattis said of leadership[30]:

"Your primary weapon is your attitude."

Well, I say make culture your primary weapon because culture is the highway to attitude, and attitude is just as effective in performance as skill.

---

30 Tom Roeder, "James Mattis Tells Air Force Graduating Class: 'Your Primary Weapon Now is Your Attitude," The Gazette. May 23 2018.

CHAPTER 4

PEOPLE

"In the Army, whenever I became fed up with meetings, protocol, and paperwork, I would rehabilitate myself with a visit to the troops."

—GENERAL DWIGHT D. EISENHOWER, 34TH PRESIDENT OF THE UNITED STATES

Now that we've established that it takes a self-leader with a vision and a commitment to culture, we turn to the pieces that fit into that culture: your people. "Invest in your people" has long been a cliché heard around businesses and organizations. However, as with most clichés, the truth behind it is often dismissed as cliché: your people are your greatest asset. This law governs business just like Newton's laws govern physics.

The clearest evidence of this truth is the Drucker Institute's Management Top 250 developed in part with the Wall Street Journal. Every year, the Drucker Institute ranks the top 250 most well-managed companies in America based on 37 objective metrics in 5 categories: employee engagement and development, financial strength, customer satisfaction, innovation, and social responsibility. Take a guess which of those 5 categories accounted most for a company's rise or fall in the rankings since 2012? You guessed it, employee engagement and development. In fact, the headline of the article itself says all you need to know: "A Company's Performance Depends First of All on Its People." A closer look at the company results revealed that the 50 biggest gainers averaged an 11.2 point increase in the employee engagement and development category.[31] For perspective, the average gains among the 50 biggest gainers in the innovation and customer satisfaction categories were 5.8 and 6.2, respectively. The authors, Rick Wartzman and Lawrence Cosby, put the data into perspective best, explaining that an 11.2 point average gain in employee engagement and development is "enough to move a company from the middle of the pack to the top 15%, or from the top 15% to the top 2%" in the overall rankings.[32] Clearly, people are your most valuable

31 Rick Wartzman and Lawrence Cosby, "A Company's Performance Depends First of All on Its People," *The Wall Street Journal*. August 12 2018.

32 Ibid.

asset. What this means for leadership is that you have to give to get. People respond best to leadership that sees them as much more than just employees, but as assets. That's why you are a leader and not a manager because no one manages assets in leadership, you employ and grow them in three main ways: Affirm, Develop, Care.

AFFIRM

On one of President Kennedy's visits to the NASA Space Center following his historic announcement that America would be going to the moon, the world learned a powerful leadership lesson about affirming your people. As the story goes, as President Kennedy walked down a hallway at the Space Center, he noticed a janitor mopping the floor of the hallway. The janitor was hard at work and the hallway was spotless.

President Kennedy stopped and shook the man's hand saying, "Hi. I'm Jack Kennedy."

The janitor introduced himself as he gladly shook President Kennedy's hand.

"What are you doing?" President Kennedy asked, expecting the janitor to explain his daily cleaning duties.

The janitor replied, "Well, Mr. President. I'm helping put a man on the moon."[33]

Clearly, this janitor had a boss who grasped the importance of affirming each individual member of the team and communicating their role's contribution to the overall mission.

Exceptional performance in any team, business, or unit arises as the result of multiple jobs being executed with commitment and an understanding of its role in the greater mission. You can probably surmise that this is difficult without self-leaders at the helm with a vision and the culture of execution to implement that vision. Once those pieces are in place, the next step of an effective leader is to affirm each and every member of the team. The leader must show not only an understanding, but also an appreciation for the work his or her teammates perform. The key is to recognize the work, not the role. No matter what role someone occupies, the mission cannot be completed without quality work executed with commitment in that role.

Think of this as a baseball team's pitching staff taking on an opponent in a baseball game. I know I often use baseball analogies, but I promise this will demonstrate the concept.

---

33 John Nemo, "What a NASA Janitor Can Teach Us About Living a Bigger Life," *The Business Journals*. December 23 2014.

The starter's role is to hold the opposing team to as few runs over as many innings as possible, being efficient and economical with pitch count. The starting pitcher's excellent work in this role, going deep into the ballgame, allowing few hits and runs, allows the specialist pitchers coming out of the bullpen to focus on only a few innings of intense, relief work. Their roles have been made easier by the starter performing excellent work in his role.

Now, the "setup man" can focus on his role—bridging the gap between starter and closer. Since the starter excelled in his role, the setup man can focus his energy on throwing exceptionally hard fastballs or crafty breaking balls for just one or two innings, putting intense care into every pitch without tiring out. The setup man's effort in his role then sets up the closer well to perform his job in the difficult role of closing out the game in the ninth inning.

The major jobs on the pitching staff are the starters and the closer—the tall, strong guys throwing smoke and wipe-out sliders who used to give me nightmares at the plate. They are the ones who earn the big bucks and have the reporters clambering for interviews after games. However, even those these team members receive most of the attention, remember that people must be affirmed and appreciated for their work and effort, not their role.

The reason being because as you saw in the pitching example, major roles only matter if excellent work is performed in supporting roles. The starter and closer have nothing to be recognized for if the middle relief and set up men don't perform well in their critical roles as well. When people sweating it out in difficult roles with little affirmation get recognition from their peers and leader, your effort to recognize their quality work ensures the person knows they are valued. Moreover, they gain an understanding that the people at the top with the vision setting the culture understand how everyone is contributing to that vision in their individual role. Your job as a leader in your team is to understand everyone's role so that you can affirm excellent work when your teammates give it. People want to go above and beyond when they know their leader is looking out for them on a consistent basis.

One of the responses I receive most often about this falls along the lines of "Well, is it really worth the time?" My core belief resides in the fact that no member of the team matters more than another. People may have different roles, but their work is just as important to the mission as the other. I adopted this belief from Joe Cohen, the legendary sports media executive, former president of the Madison Square Garden Network and former Los Angeles Kings owner.

From his early days in sports media, Joe recognized that people are the consummate asset in any business. How you treat people goes a long way in an industry like sports where the public eye is constantly focused on the teams. What would you do if I told you that not only does Joe know the name of every hot dog vender in the Garden, but also the names of the baristas in the Starbucks outside of the Garden? Sure, he knows all the suits and executives as well, but he would never pass up a chance to recognize the contributions and value of every person in the organization.[34]

Joe's secret is his personality. "I don't have a business personality and a regular personality. I'm a personal leader and I know all our employees' names and their spouses' names because you don't get the most success just trying to drive the next quarter."

What Joe's approach boils down to is the importance of dignity in how you treat people. The greatest force for creating loyalty and performance is affirming the dignity of each individual. When people feel needed by their leader, they want to fulfill that need because it's an essential component to happiness. People want to fulfill the desire to be needed, and when a leader makes clear how much they need and appreciate the contributions of their personnel, not only do they want to contribute even more, but they also achieve personal satisfaction.

---

34 Terry Lefton, "Everyone Trusts Joe," *Sports Business Journal*. March 7 2016.

In every interaction you have with your teammates, ask yourself if they have come away knowing how much they are needed and valued by you and your organization. You may say that Joe Cohen is just an anomaly, but I found this approach in many other executives through interviews, including another Cohen.

In my interview with US Marine Corps First Lieutenant Peter Cohen, who is in charge of sixty operations and maintenance Marines at Camp Pendleton, I asked Lieutenant Cohen:

"Who is the leader around whom you try to model your leadership style and why?"

Without missing a beat, Lieutenant Cohen responded: "Our Commanding Officer, Chris Hog. When it's so easy to do the bare minimum, he would wake up early and go spend time with a different unit in the battalion. He would go cook eggs with the cooks at the chow hall. Then he would go turn wrenches with the engineers for a while. He wanted to get to know every member of the battalion and understand how their role fit into our mission."

Just as with the pitching staff, the mission of this Marine battalion cannot be executed without the coordinated efforts of all members in their role. This commanding officer in charge of a battalion of a thousand Marines took the time and effort to understand each unit's responsibilities because he recognized that absent a single unit executing its role, the overall mission of combat readiness could not be accomplished. Furthermore, this commanding officer recognized the importance of recognizing how hard these Marines worked in all of those jobs, no matter how insignificant or trivial they may have seemed.

I know leadership confers significant responsibilities on an individual in addition to obligations like family, friends, exercise, and life balance. However, those teammates are your family and the five minutes it takes to acknowledge an employee or team member and their efforts pays dividends not only because it creates team chemistry, but also because it's just the right way to treat people. As a leader, do your best to make one teammate's day every single day in some small way. I promise it will improve your team's attitude and outlook.

This principle of affirmation falls back on humility. A leader without humility is a dam in leadership. It prevents so many beneficial practices from occurring. Without humility, leaders do not see a reason to get in the trenches, affirm their people, and serve alongside them. Ajay Banga, CEO of MasterCard put it best, "You can be successful without humility; but you won't enjoy it as much."[35]

35 Bill Snyder, "Mastercard CEO: Challenge Conventional Wisdom," Stanford Business School.

You would be surprised how much a leader's humility affects workplace performance. Only recently have management scientists begun to quantify humility and investigate how a leader's humility influences their teammates in challenging roles.

One recent Tsinghua University survey of over 150 frontline hospital workers connected a leader's humility to increased "deep acting" and lowered worker turnover.[36] Deep acting is the behavior in which people actively improve their own internal mood and emotions to match the collective attitude of the group. These workers were spread across thirty-three departments in everything from intense medical treatment and nursing to operating machinery.

They were all questioned about their boss's relative humility and sure enough, five months later, the departments with the most humble leaders displayed significantly lower turnover. In other words, showing your team that you are humble and right there with them in the thick of difficult assignments, no matter how challenging or bleak the situation may be, generates loyalty and trust between leader and teammates.

---

36 Jinyi Zhou and Yawen Li, "The Role of Leader's Humility in Facilitating Frontline Employees' Deep Acting and Turnover: The Moderating Role of Perceived Customer-Oriented Climate," *Journal of Leadership and Organizational Studies* Vol. 25, no. 3, 353-367.

Not only has humility in leadership been linked to lower worker turnover, but it has also been shown to have material effects on a team's performance and quality of work. A 2015 study cited in the Wall Street Journal surveyed 326 employees at a healthcare company spread across 77 teams with a wide variety of leadership styles. Interestingly, lead researcher, Bradley Owens, professor of management at Brigham Young University, concluded that "teams with humble leaders performed better and did higher quality work than teams whose leader exhibited less humility."[37] As Owens goes on to explain, "Humility is thought to enhance individual performance because admitting weaknesses highlights growth opportunities, appreciating others' strengths highlights growth exemplars, and being teachable enables personal growth to occur."[38] Professor Owens is explaining that humility is a key prerequisite for growth because it helps one recognize areas to be improved. Furthermore, humble leaders bridge the gap between leader and follower in the organizational hierarchy. Instead of hiding in their executive shell, great leaders employ humility to continuously recognize the contributions of their team and be ready to support their team however necessary.

---

37 Sue Shellenbarger, "The Best Bosses Are Humble Bosses," *The Wall Street Journal*. October 9 2018.

38 Bradley Owens and David Hekman, "How Does Leader Humility Influence Team Performance? Exploring the Mechanisms of Contagion and Collective Promotion Focus," *Academy of Management Journal* Vol. 59, no. 3, 1093.

As Marine Corps General (ret.) and Secretary of Defense James Mattis once said of his Marine Division, "Everyone fills sandbags in this uniform." In other words, any senior officer had to employ the humility to complete any job regardless of rank. In return, his Marines were motivated to accomplish any mission thrown at them. It's as simple as this. You have to give to get as a leader.

DEVELOP

It's an inevitable reality that one day we will pass on leadership to someone else within or outside our organization. Upper management decides to restructure the organization, individuals move on, or leaders get fired. Oftentimes, these occurrences happen with little notice— perhaps there is a few months-long transition period at most. However, this is simply not enough time for effective leaders to be developed from supporting roles into capable successors. Development of teammates has to be a priority not only because transitions happen suddenly, but also because more effective teammates translate into better performance.

Julie Winkle Giulioni is a renowned executive coach, author, and leader, recognized as one of Inc.'s top 100 leadership speakers. Her book, *Help Them Grow or Watch Them Go,* which she co-authored with Beverly Kaye, explores an integral, yet somewhat overlooked aspect of leadership, developing the leadership skills or subordinates. Chances are you've heard of the importance of establishing culture and self-leadership before you've heard of intentional visibility right?

Developing team members into effective leaders is a difficult task because it requires leaders to do two things: give team members tasks that usually reside on their desk and also maintain the responsibility for that task. The alternatives simply do not work. For instance, you cannot effectively develop someone into a leadership role by giving them tasks that don't matter. On the flip side, you can't give them important leadership tasks and then throw them under the bus when performance drops because they weren't ready. You cannot empower someone and then cut the floor out from underneath them. The answer to this issue in leadership is intentional visibility.

Let me tell you the story of how Julie learned this lesson and how you can implement intentional visibility into your own organization to develop those around you.

When Julie was twenty years old, she worked at a department store in Southern California. As a young, entry-level employee, she worked diligently and was hungry for more responsibility at the company. She brainstormed ways she could contribute more to the company and grow as an employee and came up with a pretty daring idea. Julie approached her boss, Mr. Kelsey, the Assistant Store Manager, explaining how she had mastered her current role and wanted to take on more at the company to grow as an employee. Mr. Kelsey was all ears but still unsure what this would look like in practice. Finally, Julie pitched him on her idea to take a leadership role on the store's new PR campaign to expand into another city nearby. This was a major request and one that Mr. Kelsey could have easily turned down given that Julie was a young employee. Instead, he found a way to say yes because he knew it would be an opportunity for Julie to grow as a teammate and leader. He granted Julie an opportunity to join the PR team on the new campaign provided she handled her other responsibilities. In short, he demonstrated the key leadership concept of intentional visibility.

Intentional visibility is the commitment to continuously expose teammates to more challenges and roles to develop them as leaders. It's the effort to show opportunities for growth through one's leadership. Remember, your team needs to make a conscious choice to follow you. You cannot achieve team excellence if they are following you because they are forced to follow you. By using intentional visibility, your team will see and take advantage of opportunities to develop themselves under your leadership, boosting confidence in you as a leader.

Surely this creates extra work for a leader. Withstanding the stress and uncertainty that comes with delegating a role to someone who has a different philosophy, approach, and qualifications as you is strenuous. But a leader must understand the long-term goals in addition to the short-term goals. The broader mission was to develop Julie to lead in this job one day even if that meant incurring some longer nights and setbacks while she was learning through the public-relations campaign and intentional visibility. Certainly, intentional visibility does not mean handing the reigns over to an intern, but it does mean revealing incrementally more responsibility and challenge to team members to keep developing them as leaders. Although the decision may have seemed risky and perhaps overbearing, Mr. Kelsey was definitely not naïve. He knew Julie was not ready for a job as consequential as this, but he kept a close eye on Julie's project.

As Julie recalled, "Mr. Kelsey was so smart because he let me go off on my own in the deep water, but he was always just close enough to come rescue me and provide some guidance if I faltered. To continue the metaphor, he dropped me in the deep end, but had the life preserver handy just in case."

Intentional visibility just comes down to opening doors for people through your leadership. If people don't see a benefit to themselves in your leadership, they will not follow wholeheartedly and performance will suffer. Imagine how

Julie would have felt if Mr. Kelsey had immediately denied her request. Instead, Mr. Kelsey found a way to honor her request for a chance to grow through more responsibility. He knew he couldn't give her the lead role on the project, but he wanted Julie to own her self-development through a new project because he could tell she was serious about learning. Mr. Kelsey's effort was matched and then some by Julie.

She explained, "Interesting work trumps compensation. Mr. Kelsey didn't have to pay me a penny more but just allowing me to do something novel and build new skills and experiences kept me engaged. And he got extra work out of me in the process!"

While Julie's experience with Mr. Kelsey in her first job may seem like a small scale example, the lesson is clear: use intentional visibility to give people a chance to grow and you'll be amazed at how much they want to work even harder and contribute even more. The principle is as true today as ever: grow your people and they will grow your company.

One complaint I hear about intentional visibility quite often is "What is the use of developing young leaders when turnover is so high among college graduates and entry level workers? Why develop people as leaders when most leave so quickly?"

This is certainly a fair question because it's not cheap in dollars or headaches training a young team member through fire and mistakes.

However, What's the alternative? Training someone as a leader has tangible and intangible benefits, even if that person never occupies a formal leadership position in your organization or any other organization. By giving team members intentional visibility, you give them a glimpse into the strategy behind what they are doing on a daily basis. Most importantly, you are placing them closer to the inner "Why" or the greater purpose of your organization. The closer people are to their mission, the greater effort they will exert in fulfilling the role they have been assigned.

Intentional visibility works in Los Angeles retail chains and also at the highest echelons of major corporations. JP Nicols, former Chief Private Banking Officer of US Bank experienced a similar story in his tenure. JP had worked in private banking since he graduated college in 1984. Seventeen years later in 2001, he had been promoted from a branch manager in Cleveland, Ohio, to Senior Vice President of the Private Client Group, leading the Cleveland office's operations.

JP did a phenomenal job turning the Cleveland office around, doubling pre-tax income, finding new markets around Cleveland, and turning the office profitable again. Undoubtedly,

JP was intelligent, diligent, and team-oriented. Although he wasn't bored in his role, an incredible leader, Londa Dewey, President of US Bank's Private Client Group, recognized JP's work within his role two rungs below her on the ladder and tapped JP for a new role through intentional visibility. She wanted JP to lead the newly established western region for the Private Client Group.

Needless to say, JP was taken aback. He would now be responsible for managing twenty-five offices in eight different states across the western continental United States. JP was understandably apprehensive and intimidated. How could he or anyone in his position be ready to tackle a new job responsible for the growth of twenty-five offices across such a wide area of the nation?

Londa knew he could never be fully prepared, but she knew at some point, JP needed to take on vacant, higher roles at the bank for his self-leadership, communication skills, and emphasis on innovation. If she wanted to retain his talent at US Bank, she had to help him grow by pushing him out of the nest and allowing him to take ownership over a role.

JP remarked, "I wasn't ready for a job like this, but Londa knew you can never really be ready. She dropped me in the deep end and kept a close eye on me. She wanted me to learn, but she wouldn't let me fail and she was a phenomenal leader for that."

JP proved to be a capable leader in the western region, empowering offices to be innovative, finding new markets within their jurisdiction and creating product development teams focused on weathering the massive disruption that technology was causing in the banking industry. His performance as manager of the western region of the Private Client Group merited a promotion to the role of Chief Private Banking Officer in 2008. However, he would have never have had a chance to develop those remarkable leadership qualities of innovation, aggressiveness, and communication across offices if Londa had not recognized the value of intentional visibility.

By bringing JP to strategy meetings and moving him into a role that would challenge him, Londa was doing him and US Bank a service. One of the ultimate failures of a leader is to keep team members in the same roles with the same tasks time after time. Excellent leaders grow their subordinates by constantly challenging them with new tasks, ideas, and roles. Intentional visibility is the mode by which leaders can reengage their team in the mission of the organization and motivate individuals to become team focused.

As Julie and JP's stories show, exceptional leaders make a commitment beyond their daily responsibilities to make sure that their followers see the potential to lead in themselves. Not only does this create better transitional leaders when leaders move onto another organization or project, but it also creates team members who are more eager to lead even if they do not occupy a formal leadership role in their organization.

But what happens if your teammates fail? No one escapes failure in their lifetime. If they did, they weren't trying hard enough. How should leadership address underperforming or failing teammates? I think the answer lies in an age old approach with a new twist.

We constantly hear the saying "Never make the mistake twice." But I think this misses the point because it makes us reluctant to take on new, challenging tasks. Here's a better approach:

1. Make as many mistakes as possible
2. Then never make the same mistake twice

Leadership should address mistakes and failure with this framework because it makes clear that being aggressive and entrepreneurial is expected, but that learning from failure is tantamount to all else. As General James Mattis has said regarding this paradox, "Expect failure, but don't accept it."[39] When a teammate fails, reaffirm how much they are needed

39 John Boitnott, "7 Leadership Lessons from U.S. Secretary of Defense James Mattis," *Entrepreneur*. March 6 2018.

by their team first and then delve into addressing what went wrong. The conversation should never digress into a finger pointing, blame game. The second this situation starts, people get defensive and you can't grow with your walls up around you.

Rather, focus on pinpointing where the error occurred and how this teammate can be prepared to attack the problem next time. As always, this teammate should never doubt how much you value and need them as a member of the team and how much you as their leader want to witness improvement. General Mattis gives another great lesson about this situation[40]:

"When a Marine or unit is screwing up, hug them more."

CARE

I am certainly not here to tell you that you need to care for your teammates as a leader. You already know how integral that is to your success. However, one of the leadership dilemmas that arose frequently in this project is how to simultaneously care for your people, but also maintain high expectations and standards? How can you be the voice of discipline and the voice of compassion? I advocate for a new

40 Ibid.

method to solve this problem that preserves performance and establishes a caring two-way relationship between leader and teammate. Approach this problem by treating your teammates like you are their parent.

Now, this does not mean you become their babysitter and caretaker. They still have to do their own homework and run their own ship. However, it does mean that when trying times arise, you treat them just as you would hope your parent would treat you. How would you like your parents to treat you in an economic recession? That's exactly how you should lead your teams when crises arise. Lead with high standards and expectations, but make abundantly clear that nothing outgrows your people. The story of a popular movie review website you have probably heard of may illustrate our approach well.

As a college student at UC Berkeley, Senh Duong launched a movie review website with his two close friends, Patrick Lee and Stephen Wang. It was in August of 1998 when the three friends realized the potential of their idea—a movie review site with opinions from tons of critics that actually gave you the real rundown of movies playing in theaters. They officially incorporated the business in January of 2000 with stunning success.[41]

---

41 Tim Ryan, "Rotten Tomatoes Oral History," Rotten Tomatoes. December 4 2009.

Lee, Duong, and Wang would go on to raise capital and build a team of 25 employees in the next several months. However, the remarkable growth they had experienced would not last. By March of 2000, the dot-com bubble had burst and global stocks had experienced their steepest decline in decades.[42] An economic downturn followed and struck the business deeply. The three young entrepreneurs immediately saw their business suffer. Even after taking several pay cuts, Lee, Duong, and Wang knew what this meant for the business—layoffs.

Lee recognized his employees were doing remarkable work marketing the site and increasing visitor traffic. But he knew they would run out of cash next year unless a miracle fell on them. Leadership met with employees and discussed the hard news, but they did it as a family and they survived because of the way they treated people with care.

Lee remarked, "We gathered everyone and basically told them we appreciated them dearly, but we just couldn't afford to keep everyone. We told them they still had a job with us right now, but that they should start looking for other employment now and we would keep them on our payroll until they found another job."

---

42 Chris Alden, "Looking Back on the Crash," *The Guardian*. March 10 2005.

In a recession, you wouldn't throw your kids out and let them go, would you? I would surely hope not although businesses are different in that layoffs are an unfortunate consequence of recessions and the business cycle. We do our best to take care of everyone, but there are times when we just cannot. Even in that situation, Lee taught us what it means to lead with care and compassion in times of crisis. He moved out of his apartment and for six months, slept on a mattress under his desk, evaded office security at night, and took no pay to support the business. Nothing would quell his passion for the product and the mission despite the circumstances. He knew that if he stayed passionate about the product and they kept building value in the site, the money would eventually come.

Rotten Tomatoes is now the most widely used movie review site in the world and worth millions of dollars.

Lee didn't have to endure sleepless nights in the office, hide from the office security guards, and keep those people on his payroll until their job search yielded new work. However, he did those things because he understood that people were his most valuable asset. He still expected the most out of his teammates in those hard times when every month stock indices and economic indicators ticked downward. But through all of that adversity, he led with compassion and treated his teammates no differently than if they were members of his own family.

Too often, we fall into the trap of thinking leadership is some function of hierarchy where some select elite get to enjoy the perks of their position. This thinking is especially prevalent in today's world with our debate over executive compensation, benefits, and perks. However, as Patrick Lee reminds us, leadership is about setting an example and serving your people from the front. People followed Patrick Lee because he was willing to give more of himself to the mission than anyone else. You can be the voice of discipline and the voice of compassion at the same time by embodying the conduct you wish to see as a leader.

Not only is it morally the right thing to do to take care of your people and treat them like you would treat your children, but it also pays dividends in performance. It's no surprise that teammates are motivated to perform for leaders whom they know care about them and the challenges they want to overcome in their lives. In its simplest form, people want to follow leaders who see them as people and not tasks or roles on the team. Chances are that you have between five and ten direct reports coming to you and one to five people to whom you report directly. This is not a great deal of people and they're a group with whom a working and also friendly relationship goes a long way. Make a conscious effort to establish regular contact with these people outside of work-related activities.

I learned the power and consequences of this leadership lesson in one of my first interviews for this project. Peter Brine is the founder and former co-owner of Brine Lacrosse, a popular lacrosse gear retail company. Their firm had a difficult start as Brine Lacrosse did not take off until over a decade after its founding.

Peter and his brother scratched and clawed for years to build the business and turn a profit similar to how Patrick Lee built Rotten Tomatoes. Looking over the financial records one day, Peter noticed that money was consistently disappearing on a biweekly basis and it was tied to one employee. Peter approached her with the suspicion that something was the matter with the missing money. Immediately the mood changed and she looked down to the right, a telltale sign of guilt.

Peter remarked, "I discovered that she was stealing money from the company and we had absolutely no idea about it. All that time, I had no clue where those discrepancies were coming from in the financials. I was furious and extremely disappointed."

I was dumbfounded as to what to say, but I sensed the tension in Peter's voice and I tried to show solidarity in his side of the story: "Being the owner of the business, I can imagine that must have been furious."

But then he said something completely remarkable I could have never anticipated him saying. I figured he would certainly give me a lecture about hiring the right people who place their integrity and the integrity of the company above all else, about maintaining discipline as a leader.

But no, instead he said to me:

"I was so furious with myself. I should have paid more attention and made the effort to get to know her and her situation. She was stealing the money because she needed it desperately for rent and food. As the leader of the company, I should have known she was in a difficult financial position and done something about it, but I did not make the effort."

As Peter learned that day, when people sign onto your team as a leader, they become family to you. Leaders can become incredibly busy and I understand how that hindered Peter from recognizing the situation. But, I promise if you maintain the conviction that teammates are family at heart, you will never be too busy to ensure they are healthy, confident, and enthusiastic.

Leadership is just as much a showcase of soft skills like compassion and friendship as it is hard skills like analysis and strategy. Patrick Lee and Peter Brine both understood the importance of placing themselves in the day-to-day lives of their teams. Although Peter learned it the hard way, they both came to understand that no leader can get the best out of a team that he or she does not understand on a personal, human, emotional level. In reality, these techniques are not rocket science, but they just require an immense amount of effort. But as Peter explained to me, you have to understand your team to know how to utilize their talents best and grow them.

Remember, what you put into your most valuable asset, your people, you will get out of them. As President Kennedy, Joe Cohen, Lieutenant Cohen, Julie Winkle Giulioni, Patrick Lee, and Peter Brine all demonstrated, if you give your people the right fuel, attention, and resources and you will be impressed by how much they give back to you, their leader. Affirm, develop, and care for your people and they will affirm, develop, and care for you, your leadership, and your organization.

CHAPTER 5

SERVE

"It's an honor and a privilege to lead your Marines."

—FIRST LIEUTENANT PETER COHEN, USMC

"My number one belief about leadership is that you are a servant first and foremost."

—TONY ROBBINS

"If anyone be great amongst you, let him be your servant."

—JESUS CHRIST

The concept of service in leadership may turn some leaders away. Some say that service is preposterous. Great leaders deliver results—record earnings reports, excellent grades, battles and elections won. I want a sense of accomplishment and respect in my leaders, not a sense of indebtedness or servitude. However, this thinking is precisely the thinking that turns potential leaders into counterproductive micromanagers. Exceptional leaders achieve great results not because they pursue them, but because these results ensue from serving and focusing on people. In essence, they achieve magnificently because they make clear that their leadership is not about them, but about who they are and how they treat their teams.

If leaders receive power from the members of their team, and then just focus on maintaining that power to support their image and authority, the team loses its trust in that leader. They will cease granting their leader influence, and a leader without influence is a ship without sails. In other words, if leaders are entrusted with such power and then turn around and focus the mission on them and not their team, they lose credibility, trust, and engagement from their employees. The loss of trust is a two-way street as leaders then abandon their faith in their teams and resort to micromanagement to achieve their results.

So often I hear the response that service in leadership is misguided because leaders are heroes. I see where people are coming from with this sentiment, but there is a fundamental misunderstanding here. Leaders are not heroes, but leaders create heroes. Without Abraham Lincoln, there is no Ulysses Grant. Without Jesus, there are no twelve disciples. Without Franklin Delano Roosevelt, there is no General and President Eisenhower.

We may conceive of leaders as heroes because they played a role in heroic achievements like saving the Union or Europe, but notice how much these leaders drove people to accomplish heroic feats. Why did people choose to follow these people? Because they recognized that leadership wasn't about them, but serving their people. We want to be the hero, solve the problems, initiate the change, and save the day, but in the end, our egos want this, not the leader within us. Egos want recognition, but leaders want victories.

The leader wants to find a way to put their team in a position to solve the problem, not to necessarily solve every problem themselves. It is not a sign of incapability or laziness, but rather an example of awareness and inspiration to know that one cannot try to be a hero and a leader at the same time. Don't focus on being a hero. Rather, focus on creating heroes by developing and serving your teammates.

When leaders recognize this central fact about leadership—that it's not about them, but who they are—they realize that not only is leadership a choice, but more importantly, followership is a choice too. Your people have to choose to follow you and become worthy of that choice and trust through service. Famous leadership author and speaker Peter Anderton sums up servant leadership best: "It's all about choice. But, it's not your choice. It's their choice!" This is leadership: when the team opts to grant the leader power because they make it about the team, not themselves, through service.

I had the privilege to interview Angie Morgan for this project, a renowned leadership keynote speaker, retired US Marine Corps Officer, and coauthor of *Spark: How to Lead Yourself and Others to Greater Success.* Lieutenant Morgan served as a public affairs officer in the Marine Corps for eight years. During her time in the Marines she learned the organization's "service-based leadership" model, implementing this style at every rank throughout her career. She retired from the Marine Corps in 2005 to cofound her leadership consulting company, Lead Star, with her Marine Corps colleague, Courtney Lynch.

She told me a remarkable story about how as a young lieutenant in basic infantry training she learned to lead people and expect the most out of them, while still being the officer who cared most about them. For six months, she and her fellow trainees were under the command of Captain Harper, a short, but strict cannonball of a Marine drill instructor.

According to Lieutenant Morgan, "He was only five-foot-four, but no one ever told him that. He walked around like he was seven feet tall."

He was a tough, stern, unforgiving leader. When he entered a room, a cold aura of seriousness and hierarchy followed closely.

Mrs. Morgan recounted that, "He scared me to death. He called himself Coca-Cola because he was the 'real thing.'"

Routinely, Marines were held extremely accountable and paid the price for failing to meet Captain Harper's standards and expectations.

Mrs. Morgan remarked, "I thought, I want to make sure that he never sees me make a mistake. But one day, I was sitting in class and our instructor had a note passed to him. He opened it, read it, and pointed to me saying, 'Hey, Lieutenant, you need to go down and see Captain Harper immediately.' And in an instant, my heart sank to my stomach. It felt as though I had been physically punched in the gut."

"All I could think about was what did I do? Even twenty years later, I remember just how scared I was, the nerves and trepidation, but I reported."

Captain Harper said, "Angie, sit down."

Angie noted a difference in Captain Harper's tone right when she sat down in his office. She had never heard this tone from him before, but it sounded oddly like compassion.

He said, "Angie, I have some really sad news I have to tell you. I just got off the phone with your mother and your grandmother has just passed away. What can I do to get you home right now to be with your family?"

Angie could not find words to answer Captain Harper's question.

Captain Harper then continued, "Well let me tell you what I've already done. There's a ticket waiting for you at Washington Reagan Airport. I called your parents to let them know when you're going to be arriving home. I have a colleague outside the door and he's going to take you to your apartment and then to the airport after you've packed. I called your training officer and let him know what's going on and he will be fine with your absence. And, Angie, this Marine Corps, it's an interesting organization. I don't know how we've done it, but somehow we have succeeded for 225 years without you. You're going to be off for a couple of weeks, but don't worry about it, we will still be alright without you."

This moment was nothing short of astounding. Mrs. Morgan was certainly in much disbelief and mourning the loss of her grandmother. However, Captain Harper, this hardened, disciplined Marine drill instructor made of steel, showed a side of compassion that Lieutenant Morgan and her fellow trainees had not experienced thus far in their training. After receiving physical punishment and mental stress from this instructor for so many weeks, to see him exhibit compassion and emotion was revolutionary.

Lieutenant Morgan arrived at home and detailed that "It was a wonderful reunion with my family, but right behind me when I arrived was a knock on the door. A flower delivery man appeared with the largest bouquet of flowers that I have ever seen in my entire life. I opened up the card attached and of course it was from Captain Harper and my colleagues at the Basic School."

She would go on to explain that "To be a leader, you can be tough, have standards, and hold people accountable to them, but if at the end of the day, you're not serving them, you're never going to be able to build a team where they will be there for you in the thick of a fight."

Leadership is so often misconstrued as someone rising above the rest in knowledge, experience, discipline, and bravery, Lieutenant Morgan's initial impression of Captain Harper.

However, we neglect the emotional side of leadership where leaders truly engage with a follower or team member. How useful is a completely invulnerable, inhuman leader to whom you cannot relate in the slightest? Leadership is the art of bringing out the best in people and creating the strongest of bonds between the members of a team because ultimately, the team accomplishes the mission, not you.

After eight years in the Marine Corps, Mrs. Morgan believes that the Marines have the highest percentage of members in any organization nationwide who get the logo of their organization tattooed on themselves. What is it about the Marine Corps that motivates so many Marines to get the Eagle, Globe, and Anchor tattooed on themselves? When is the last time you saw someone at the beach with Goldman Sachs or McKinsey & Co. tattooed to their arm? The answer is the servant-based leadership model that Lieutenant Morgan and the Marine Corps implement in training and deployment. No rank and file member of a team is motivated to contribute to a leader if that connection is a one-way street. People decide to put the organization ahead of themselves when they know their leader works to serve and protect them, not extract from them.

It may seem counterintuitive at first, but teammates who feel served and therefore valued by their organization in turn desire to serve their organization or employer even more.

Servant leadership does not need to be major, grandiose acts either. In fact, even the most subtle acts of service and gratitude from the leader of a team can create the tight bonds between leader and team that produce remarkable results. For example, watch Drew Brees get in the huddle with his offense. Brees is among the shortest quarterbacks in football. Yet, his teammates respect and trust his skills on the field because of his self-leadership, vision, and competitive edge. However, there is one more thing Brees does regularly that exemplifies servant leadership on the field. He kneels before his teammates in the huddle.

One could surmise that the quarterback is the leader because he's the one the media focus on relentlessly, who gets paid the most, and is often involved in the scoring. But, Brees is the leader of the New Orleans Saints because he earns leadership from his teammates by serving them. Kneeling before his teammates as he delivers the play in the huddle, he makes it abundantly clear that he understands his teammates matter more to him than anything else and that he needs each and every one of them to score.

Immediately, his teammates feel valued beyond the role they play on the field. Stepping onto the football field is a dangerous endeavor, especially for an entire season. Quarterbacks are protected at all costs by the other ten players on the field. But, Brees illustrates by kneeling in the huddle that his teammates are the heart and soul of the offense. As a result, they perform exceptionally well for him and it's no surprise Brees now holds the record for most passing yards in the NFL.[43]

It's precisely the same concept Jesus displayed before his twelve disciples. Jesus was the epitome of a servant leader, a leader who is still widely followed two millennia after his passing. Jesus' disciples were dumbfounded when he ordered them to rest and let him wash their feet. They figured Jesus was the leader and deserved to have his own feet washed by his followers. But Jesus turned their perspective around completely, serving them first by washing their feet, the universal sign of respect, care, and service in those days. You may say, well that doesn't matter, it just upsets the power structure that drives our output as an organization.

One response I hear often is this: "I get what you're saying, but I don't need to serve my teammates to make them know what to do. I don't need them to love me. I need them to perform for me."

I understand where this sentiment comes from, yet I think it misses the point. Teammates who are served by their leaders understand on a deeper level that they are valued beyond

---

43 Chris Graythen, "Drew Brees Breaks All-Time Passing Yard Record," CBS News. October 9 2018.

the work they do for their leader. They understand that their leader has the best interest of his or her people in mind at all times. In other words, servant leadership creates intrinsic motivation. The care for a person on an emotional level creates a deep-seated bond of indebtedness and respect from follower to leader.

You need people to want to follow you, not have to follow you through hierarchy. People only want to follow people who value them on an intrinsic level. Furthermore, people only listen to one radio station: WIIFM 24.7. What's in it for me twenty-four hours a day seven days a week. Great leaders recognize this underlying facet of human nature and create a want to follow in their teammates through alignment. I call this aligning for growth, wherein leaders align the personal goals of their teammates with those of the team. In this fashion, teammates see a path forward for themselves through following one's leadership.

Unfortunately, we have been conditioned to think that leadership is all about the leader and their unique talents, rather than their team's abilities. Interestingly, most people know this when you ask them. No one admittedly says that leadership is all about the leader, their power, and their capabilities relative to the team. Yet, how many of you have had a coach, boss, or other leader turn the objective into their own mission and let their ego and personal agenda take over the team and the mission? We are consciously ignorant of how we conflate leadership with power rather than empowerment. The root of empowerment is service, an idea we do not often associate with leadership because we think leadership is about being a superhero.

Jeff Proctor may well be a superhero, but he leads like a servant. Jeff is the president of Pro Angle Media, the sports media production company that covers all of the Dodgers, Lakers, Kings, and Angels games. He's one of the most successful and networked sports media executives in Los Angeles, but if you observe the way he walks around the office, stadium, or arena, you would think he's just your regular guy and sports fan. Here's how he and his team have achieved such remarkable success.

Every employee who walks into the office is Jeff's mission. Each event Pro Angle covers is not primarily an event to make money for the firm or further cement their brand, but another chance to develop his people. Everything Jeff does is centered around his people. In fact, barring a serious lunch meeting, Jeff spends lunch every day with Pro Angle interns, focusing on how Pro Angle can create a stepping stone for them into their dream job.

In fact, in our interview, Jeff told me that his proudest leadership moment was when his executive producer took her dream job at her alma mater, but could not hold back tears because of how much Jeff employed servant leadership. I know this isn't always possible for executives, but think about the small things you can do to put your people first and how they will improve your people's experience. Remember, leadership is not about expanding your dominion. Leadership is about expanding your service and going beyond the call of duty.

Jeff doesn't stop here. He recognized early in his career that service in leadership ultimately comes back to creating a bond between leader and follower. People follow leaders with whom they can relate. It's tough to relate to a leader wearing a designer suit on vacation in the Maldives so Jeff erases every barrier to a relationship between his people and him. He does this because he knows they will only want to follow someone to whom they can relate.

"I don't drive a Rolls Royce. I drive a Ford Fusion and I don't care. I want my people to drive Rolls Royces! What's everyone going to think when we hit tough times and I stroll into work in a Rolls Royce?"

Think of it this way. Jeff sees his job as manager of all these employees as a responsibility to make them better by serving their needs. That Pro Angle is profitable and growing serves as proof that he is serving employees well and that service from leadership is manifesting itself in the bottom line.

We are in the midst of a national debate right now about long-term vs short-term results in companies and beefing up the bottom line for the earnings report. Instead of picking a side, think of this for a change. The quickest way to impact your bottom line is to earn the hearts and admiration of your people. As Jeff has displayed throughout his career, if you want to win, start by serving your people.

CHAPTER 6

FEEDBACK

"Feedback is the breakfast of champions."

—KEN BLANCHARD

"Criticism, like rain, should be gentle enough to nourish a man's growth without destroying his roots."

—FRANK A. CLARK

Thrive on feedback in everything you do as a leader, parent, spouse, and teammate. Think of your organization as a sports car. If people are your fuel and leadership is your GPS, feedback is a nitro boost. However, many people I have spoken to consider feedback to be an uncomfortable concept. Instead of utilizing feedback as a year-round process, they fear it like a trip to the dentist. They consider feedback to be a trip to the body shop instead of a boost to performance. Much of this misconception about feedback's role in an organization stems from the way we insert our egos into our leadership. When this misconception arises, it often appears as a result of thinking feedback is a leader versus teammate interaction. In reality, feedback is an all of us as a team versus the problem interaction.

RECEIVING FEEDBACK

Receiving feedback may be among the toughest tasks you encounter as a leader. What makes receiving feedback so difficult is that you feel as though people don't understand how difficult your job is as a leader and don't take that into account when giving their criticism. However, the way around this problem is to refer back to the self-leadership we talked about in chapter 1. Excellent self-leaders check their ego and understand that feedback is not a criticism or insult, but rather an asset.

I understand that it's hard to accept feedback because oftentimes it is directing you toward problems you were not aware of in your team and may be ashamed of, but you have to look at feedback as the first step in addressing those problems. People only give feedback because they care enough about their fellow teammates and leaders to give it. The next time you receive feedback from a teammate or boss, challenge yourself to check your feelings and recognize that feedback, even if highly critical, as a sign of an investment in you as an individual.

The summer after my freshman year of college, I worked an internship at a small investment banking firm and my manager was a feedback hawk. I had the least experience of all the interns in the firm given that I was only a sophomore and lacked the business classes they had taken. My manager, a machine-like second year analyst, quickly hit me with some discouraging feedback, but he did it the right way.

He took me out to lunch, away from the office and our workload. He basically told me to my face that day that I was doing terribly: "We need to get your work quality up because it's causing more work for the associates."

That sure sucked to hear and it was a blow to my confidence. However, even though I wasn't a leader at this firm, I did my best to exhibit the self-leadership necessary to recognize that my manager who had tons of other things to be doing, took the time to give me feedback so I could improve. He would never have done that if he thought I was a lost cause. The challenge is to get over the initial frustration of having your ego suffer and see feedback as others investing in you. Even if you feel as though you're doing fantastic work in your role, no one is perfect.

Instead of becoming frustrated that you aren't perfect or haven't met your own standards, control your emotions enough to use feedback to get back in the game and prove yourself to your leaders and teammates. Think of this way, receiving feedback is like a mechanic trying to work on a car's engine or change the oil. Can you imagine trying to change the oil or fix the engine with the hood down? That's essentially what you are doing when you become defensive in feedback interactions.

As with most everything in leadership, approach receiving feedback as a way to lead by example. When your teammates see you and the brass taking feedback like adults and using it to improve your performance and therefore their work lives also, they follow that example. More importantly, they appreciate that effort on your part because it shows a consistent effort to improve your leadership such that they can be developed by a better leader on a daily basis.

As a leader, you earn extra collective buy-in from your teammates when you receive feedback in stride because people want to work for a leader whom they know they can communicate with and will respond to their input. Oftentimes, your teammates are closer to the friction areas of your business because they are lower down the hierarchy. Communicating and receiving feedback from them positively is a sure way to improve trust and performance. If you're still unsure, ask yourself this. If my leader is responsible for my family as in the case of a job, or my life as in the case of the military, do I want that person to be more or less open to receiving and utilizing feedback through communication?

Receiving feedback positively is also a function of how you've built and trained your teammates in your organization. If you have a quality group of people led by a servant and self-leader with a vision and strong culture, people will understand how to receive and employ feedback. In other words, if you've been doing your job, your example will be enough to ensure people are utilizing feedback properly.

GIVING FEEDBACK

The simplest way to approach giving feedback is to imagine the way in which you would like to receive feedback. However, this may lead people to sugarcoat the issue or run aground for fear of hurting their teammate or leader's feelings. We can't be afraid of stepping on people's toes when giving feedback. After all, what's the use in giving feedback if you're just going to sugarcoat the problem in your conversation. The point of feedback is to attack the problem, not hint at it.

Instead of sugarcoating, I encourage you to give feedback in the context of a relationship with your leader or your teammates. Feedback should be relational, not transactional. One college executive I spoke to employs a strategy that I think works exceptionally well in creating a relational feedback exchange. Give feedback over lunch, coffee, or something non-work related. He never brings his employees into his office for feedback because that immediately sets off the alarm in their heads.

The first thing people think about when they get summoned to their boss or coach's office for a feedback or performance meeting is "O dear, what did I do wrong? I need to start preparing myself to defend my conduct and value to this team."

This is where the situation goes wrong because feedback cannot be a defensive mechanism. You want to create an environment where the feedback you give is likely to be received and implemented, not deflected for the sake of ego. Conducting performance reviews in an open, respectful, mentorship interaction increases the likelihood that the feedback you give will be used to improve performance. Let me give you an example of a company thriving on feedback that I think you'll recognize.

Godiva Chocolatier is one of the most widely known and successful chocolate brands with over 600 shops worldwide and operations in the United States, Europe, Japan, and China. [44]However, Godiva's story was not always so rosy. The company was facing tough times in the mid-2000s, when sales were down and the company was losing profitability. The situation worsened to the point where Campbell's Soup, Godiva's owner since 1967 decided to sell Godiva to a private equity firm in December of 2007.[45]

Enter Rich Keller, a marketing guru and Godiva's Global Vice President of Branding, Strategy, and Innovation. His title makes him sound like he isn't open to feedback right? But Rich's ability to check his company's and his own ego to utilize rather than antagonize feedback saved Godiva and created a brand new multi-million-dollar business line for Godiva.

Rich pored over Godiva's sales data in the summer of 2008, his first year at the firm. What was preventing Godiva from pushing into the next level as a company? The chocolate was high quality, the supply chain was efficient, and there was a considerable market for the product. In trying to formulate a marketing plan for senior management, Rich did what he had always done as a marketer at Nabisco and Bare Necessities—go back to the consumer. While the C-Suite became

44 "History of Godiva," Godiva Chocolatier. September 18 2007.
45 "Ulker Group to Buy Campbell's Godiva," Just-Food. December 21 2007.

frustrated with the lackluster, average performance of the company, Rich focused his team on relearning what the consumer wanted from them.

After talking to hundreds of customers and conducting focus groups, Rich and his team understood the problem. Godiva is a luxury brand. It's the chocolate of indulgence, fit for the royal family, and every ounce of their marketing reflects this persona. But how many royal families will swear allegiance to Godiva chocolate? And even then, most of Godiva's annual sales occur in the eight weeks between Thanksgiving and the end of the holiday season. How many people will buy Godiva chocolate year around? The problem became crystal clear. Godiva was aiming at too narrow of a market and no one in key management roles had accepted the feedback to fix the problem right before their eyes.

As Rich put it to me, "We were never going to win as a brand if we didn't expand Godiva outside of the mall. Nobody gets up in the morning and says to their significant other, 'I'll be back in twenty minutes. I'm going to the mall to get some truffles.'"

Rich and his team recognized they needed to meet the consumer where they were if Godiva was to reach the next echelon as a company. Researching further, Rich realized that Godiva didn't sell a single wrapped chocolate. Any and all chocolate Godiva sold was packaged in a box, further alienating the average consumer not looking for the high end chocolate line. Instead of pouting about the negative outlook like many of Godiva's leaders around him, Rich got to work on developing this new product.

Rich had no budget or support for this new line, but as a cancer survivor and marathon runner, Rich would simply not be stopped. He and his wife developed a wrapped chocolate brand in his garage.

"The goal was to bring Godiva into grocery stores, and let me tell you the pain and pushback we had: 'You're going to kill the brand' 'We're high end.'"

But again, Rich saw the value in feedback. He would frequently run focus groups and bring the CEO of Godiva to observe. Time and again, focus group after focus group, consumers showed mass support for a wrapped Godiva chocolate for the everyday person. Ten years later, it is abundantly clear that Rich and his team proved the C-Suite wrong.

Godiva Gems is now a several hundred-million-dollar business line for Godiva and any consumer can find Godiva chocolates in a grocery store. In fact, Rich's story came full circle when his daughter brought home a wrapped Godiva chocolate on Halloween.

Hundreds of millions of dollars' worth of business were generated in one man's garage because he was willing to accept feedback. While the company's leaders spun their tires trying to neglect the feedback or utilize the feedback and also maintain the status quo, Rich used it to his advantage. Remember, feedback is not you versus me. It's us versus the problem and you cannot fix problems if you're uncomfortable with change. Rich turned feedback toward the problem, leaving ego and frustration out of the game plan.

I heard a story about a retail chain owner in the course of this project who was having trouble utilizing feedback. This particular gentleman was getting plenty of feedback from his suits, the MBAs in the conference room analyzing data and sales models. These folks were convinced the next sales or margin breakthrough lay in the next model or survey. However, this owner just couldn't take the data overload anymore.

So he took the Friday off and left the office for a while. He dropped the suit and tie for some faded jeans and cattle rancher hat and took a seat at the counter of his local diner in Rogers, Arkansas to understand his customers and their shopping needs. His MBAs and VPs told him big box retail stores in small towns would never produce enough sales to be profitable. However, over time as this man took off Fridays to sit with the everyday people in their region, he learned that big box retail actually met the interests of customers in small towns. These everyday people gave him feedback on his idea to open up big box retail stores closer to their homes rather than in major cities. As it turns out, enough people loved the prospect of having their goods more readily available in bulk at cheap prices to make the model profitable, contrary to the speculation of the MBAs and VPs.

Unfortunately, Sam Walton is no longer with us, but Walmart remains one of the most successful big box retailers today because they utilized feedback to meet the customers' needs. All companies want customer feedback these days. In fact, many pay large sums of money to obtain feedback data. However, what distinguishes Sam Walton and Walmart is that they didn't stay in the office and google their customers. Rather, they left their cocoon to understand them on a deeper level so they could better serve their needs.

To understand the problems of your business or any organization, it is imperative for leaders to get into the mix where the rubber hits the road and see the problem from an outside perspective. The first step in accomplishing this is to change our outlook on feedback. Remember, view feedback as an asset and not a trip to the dentist's office, and you'll be surprised how many doors you unlock for your organization.

CHAPTER 7

COMMUNICATE

"The art of communication is the language of leadership."

—JAMES HUMES, PRESIDENTS EISENHOWER, REAGAN, AND BUSH'S SPEECHWRITER

It was a hot summer day in New York and young Allen Haines had just finished his junior year of college. Interested in film and theatre, Allen set his sights on the illusive entertainment industry. He scratched and clawed at the industry for quite some time until he finally met Eddie Davis. Mr. Davis was the general manager of Broadway back in the day, in charge of some major performances on the grandest stage in theatre. As general manager, Mr. Davis was responsible for the money and business side of the productions.

Now an accomplished Hollywood executive, former CEO of three separate production companies, and cofounder of Blue Circle Leadership, a premier leadership consulting firm, Allen owes his success to his first boss, Mr. Davis. Allen credits his leadership style to Mr. Davis, a style he has used to build companies that have marketed some of the most impressive films to date, including *Star Wars* and *Indiana Jones.*

Every day, Allen would observe Mr. Davis and his leadership style, taking note especially of how he interacted with people as their boss. Mr. Davis had all the power in the world in these theatres. After all, he was responsible for the financials of these high stakes, Broadway performances that draw the most important patrons in the industry. He had a great deal to be proud of and a great deal at stake in every performance the theatres undertook. However, as Allen took note throughout his summer working in the theatre, Mr. Davis took special care to understand how his interactions with regular rank and file team members were experienced. In essence, Allen learned how an effective leader communicates.

All leaders are ultimately real people just like the rest of us. They just have roles that oftentimes give them serious power. The important insight is that Mr. Davis never let power or prestige affect his ability to communicate as a leader. As we saw in chapters 2 and 3, people move into leadership roles because their teammates choose to follow their vision and culture. However, even the best vision and culture is useless unless it can be communicated effectively. Lose the ability to communicate and you've lost your ability to influence people as a leader.

Allen told me a beautiful story about an interaction he had with Mr. Davis and his remarkable understanding of communication as a leader. One day, Allen got a chance to finally see Mr. Davis' office for the first time when Mr. Davis asked Allen to come up to his office for a check-in meeting. It was absolutely beautiful and fitting for a Broadway executive—decked out with theater memorabilia and mementos from famous shows.

However, one object in particular caught Allen's eye, the full size mirror sitting exactly perpendicular to Mr. Davis' desk. Allen had no idea what this mirror was for and in fact, he found it somewhat creepy. The mirror was placed right next to them such that any look to their left cast their reflections right back at them. At the end of the meeting, Allen gathered the courage to ask his boss the purpose of the mirror. Mr. Davis' face lit up at the question as he saw an opportunity to explain part of his leadership philosophy to Allen through the mirror.

Mr. Davis told Allen that the mirror was placed there so that whenever Mr. Davis had someone in his office, he had a way to immediately see how his body language and expressions looked to the person to whom he was speaking. In essence, Eddie placed that mirror there to have instant feedback on how his input and vision were being received, not just how they were being communicated.

Communication is often mischaracterized as the practice of sending information. It's the idea that you have to say the right thing in the right way to set in motion what you want done. This is true, but the error lies in the fact that the leader believes what they are saying makes perfect sense to everyone. Thus, leaders are shocked when information is miscommunicated and goals are not met. It's the classic game of telephone. Everything sounds perfect going out, but receiving is where errors arise. Remember, if you've established a culture of execution, most problems come down to communication and therefore, it's especially important to achieve effective communication. The integral aspect of Mr. Davis' communication techniques, including his mirror, is that he spent more time focusing on how what he was saying was received than enjoying giving orders. As a leader, if you focus on reception more than transmission, you will automatically communicate your vision and culture more effectively.

Think about some of the greatest leaders in history. I come up with Abraham Lincoln, Winston Churchill, Martin Luther King, Jr., Ronald Reagan, and Margaret Thatcher.

What did all of these leaders have in common? They were all known for their speeches! The Gettysburg Address, The Speech Before the House of Commons, I Have A Dream!, The Speech at the Brandenburg Gate, and The Iron Lady Speech, respectively, were among the most famous speeches ever given. President Reagan was even nicknamed "The Great Communicator."

All of these leaders had remarkable visions—to save the Union, to save Europe, to secure civil rights, and to defeat the Soviet Union—but their visions would not have mattered if they lacked the ability to communicate them.

I do not pretend for a second to know how to speak like these legends, but I can convey the importance of communication and some strategies for communicating more effectively with your teams.

COMMUNICATE WITH OWNERSHIP AND INSPIRATION

As a leader, when you communicate with your team, own what you are saying and believe in the purpose of your task. A manager who tells someone what to do without believing in the mission is a boss. The manager who communicates the task to teammates with conviction and belief in the task's purpose is a leader.

One of the most demoralizing, deflating phrases in organizational management is "Management wants this done." The second a leader utters this phrase, they have lost their team's confidence and followership. By uttering this phrase, the leader has committed two cardinal mistakes of leadership—abandoning responsibility and failing to communicate the greater purpose of the mission. It's as if you didn't want to do this particular job, so you decided it would be better if someone else had to do it instead of you. This is the thinking of a boss, not a leader. All of the work it takes to earn trust through self-leadership and establish a culture and vision around your people is undermined if a leader does not communicate with conviction. What you have essentially told your teammates is that you do not believe in what they have to do and you want the responsibility for the team's performance to fall on someone else.

No one is motivated by a leader who will not take ownership over their team and who obviously does not believe in their mission. In these situations, the leader must understand the greater purpose behind the mission even if they do not agree with it and preserve the culture of execution around the team to put that mission into action. If your team does not understand the why behind their mission, they will not be motivated to put their full effort into accomplishing the what of the mission.

A leader approaches this situation through the eyes of the receiver, taking notice of how their words will be received and how that will translate into success on the job. Your job is not just to delegate, but to inspire. When you communicate tasks to people, they should want to run through a wall to accomplish that task for you because you inspired them. When assigning roles and responsibilities, take the extra second to highlight why you chose someone for a certain job and what skills they will bring that are important to the overall purpose behind the mission. The concept behind this practice is a major theme of this book: leaders inspire and bosses delegate.

There's nothing wrong with being a boss. Tasks will be accomplished and moderate success may be achieved, but true excellence, where both people and organization grow immensely cannot be achieved this way. Instead, always communicate two things when assigning tasks: the contribution of this task to the mission and the skills this teammate has that will make this task a success.

Remember, your job is to inspire, not merely delegate.

KEEP IT SIMPLE

As Tony Robbins once famously said, "Complexity is the enemy of execution." Truer words have never been spoken.

When leaders communicate simply, it's not a signal of being condescending toward teammates. Rather, it's a sign of respect and belief in their capabilities.

When a leader communicates a task to a teammate in a long-winded fashion with multiple variables and set in stone procedures, they cloud the agenda of their teammate. Furthermore, they show a lack of trust in the teammate—as if this person could not complete their task without the leader's micromanagement.

Not only is this counterproductive because the teammate has an overloaded agenda, but also because they clearly know their leader is sweating the prospect of delegating this task to them. In short, when you communicate with complexity, you implicitly communicate a lack of confidence. If leaders don't communicate with confidence, they stand little chance of inspiring their people.

Instead, communicate to spark the creativity of your people and their skills. When delegating tasks, give the overall objective of your teammate's task, including its contribution to the greater mission and the importance of their unique skills. Let them know what absolutely must be done in simple terms, and then trust your people enough to use their skills and creativity to accomplish the task.

Certainly, this does not mean leaders should not provide some suggestions or past experiences. However, it does mean one should be aware of how their words are perceived. Communicating with complexity usually happens under one's radar. It's integral to recognize whether one's communication inspires through simplicity or clouds through complexity.

LISTEN MORE THAN YOU SPEAK

While much of leadership is perceived as people giving orders down the chain of command, it's imperative to recognize that these directives are based on information coming up the chain of command. People whose voices are heard are valued people, and people who feel valued want to perform even more for a leader. However, when people see a leader intent on mostly giving out information or hearing themselves speak, people begin to lose trust in and respect for that person.

Although this may sound like chapter 6: Feedback, in reality, it's about chapter 1: Self-Leadership. A self-confident, reassured leader does not feel the need to always be the one calling the shots in the meetings or always hearing their voice tower above the others. Rather, these self-leaders recognize the immense value in the people they've hired and the limitations of their own abilities. They don't feel the need to always prove their worth in their role by giving orders or dominating meetings. Instead, these leaders listen. They listen to learn and they listen to value. When a person in a position of leadership becomes close-minded, their teammates feel less motivated to contribute because they no longer own the mission—they just work for the firm.

Overall, remember that communication is a tool to be developed just like any other tool such as culture, strategy, vision, and self-leadership. Not only is communication a tool, but it is also a door to be unlocked toward growth. Information is worth its weight in gold in today's economy. The more leaders practice communicating important information through conviction, simplicity, and purposeful listening, the greater chance they will have at success in today's world. The best way to approach communication is to always make sure the other person walks away from the conversation feeling informed, valued, and confident.

CHAPTER 8

DON'T PUSH, PULL

"Leadership without ego is the rarest, yet most valuable commodity we have."

—BOB DAVIDS

If you've ever played 20Q and wondered how the hell that little device knew you were thinking about sub-saharan zebras, you have Radica Games to thank for that. Founded in 1983, Radica was the third most profitable electronic toy producer behind Mattel and Hasbro until its sale to Mattel.[46] In 1998, Radica stunned analysts by becoming the most profitable toy company in the world, a title that either Mattel or Hasbro had

46 Dan Burrows, "Mattel Buys Radica for $230 Million," Market Watch. July 26 2006.

held for years. How did a smaller, younger toy company steal so much market share from the titans of the toy industry?

I sat down with Bob Davids, former Radica CEO, renowned leadership author, and speaker to discuss Radica's success and his approach to managing this remarkable turnaround.

And he immediately corrected me. "Leadership isn't management because management is control. Management is the control, the interplay of time, quality, and money. So where are people? Well, people come under leadership."

By no means does it suffice to say that management is to be disregarded. Time, quality, and money are all real concerns in any business, organization, or military unit. Leaders have to know their technicals and understand the operations of an organization to develop strategy. However, management and leadership are two different practices that those in power must distinguish from each other. Management entails decision-making while leadership requires unification around that decision and overall goal.

Davids changed the way I think about leadership fundamentally by explaining how managers make decisions but leaders unify a team:

"Managers push people, but leaders pull people."

People are the lifeblood of any organization, but a leader cannot push them. Rather the leader must create an environment where people are motivated. It's almost impossible to motivate someone as a leader— you cannot make someone want something that they do not want. Despite this situation, it's still the job of the leader to create an environment where effort is rewarded by pulling them rather than pushing them toward the goal. Davids has built six different successful companies and he attributes this success to how he leads people by pulling them toward the goal rather than pushing them toward it from behind.

Interestingly, he learned the importance of this goal when one of a leader's most important assets, communication, was gone. As a young executive in China, he was on a run when he noticed a peculiar sight down to the right of the road. A team of workers was placing a drainage pipe underground, but Davids noticed something was terribly wrong as he stopped to investigate. The workers were laying the pipe exactly parallel to the ground, meaning gravity wouldn't pull the water down the pipe and it would be defective. Davids hollered out to the men, but immediately realized they couldn't understand his English.

Little did Davids know, but he was about to learn a foundational leadership principle. Davids needed to get down in the trench and pull the team toward the goal, showing them that the pipe needed to be tilted, rather than directing from the street above. When you push people, you have no idea where they will go. But, when you position yourself between the team and the team's goal, pulling them toward it, you communicate an incredibly effective and contagious vision and confidence to them.

So Davids removed his shoes, climbed down into the muddy ditch and started pulling. He transcended the language barrier between him and his team through his example. He picked up a pebble and motioned how the pebble wouldn't roll down the pipe if it was parallel to the ground. Immediately, the team understood the situation and the overall goal—to set a tilted pipe. Davids helped them position a few rocks underneath one side of the pipe so that it would have a slight tilt. Since Davids pulled the team toward the goal, the team had been drawn toward their objective and closer to their leader, not pushed toward it and farther from their leader, even though they spoke different languages.

Davids attributes this key leadership insight to "Eisenhower's Chain." During World War II, General Eisenhower, Supreme Commander of the Allied Expeditionary Force would explain leadership with a chain. Not just any chain, though. This chain was long and composed of large, heavy, steel links. Eisenhower would pile the chain up in a large heap, bring in his generals from many different Allied nations, and ask them a simple question. If I push this chain over right now, which way will it go? The generals would ponder the pile of individual links chained together and how their movements would affect one another, but they ultimately knew there could be no answer. There were just too many variables in how a push might affect the chain's posture.

Eisenhower would recognize their indecision and explain that there really is no answer. Eisenhower wanted his generals to understand that just as he pushed the chain over, if they pushed their soldiers, there was no telling where they would go or how they would perform. The key was to pull them using their example as leaders.

Eisenhower continued, "But, if I pick up the end of the chain and pull it rather than push the pile, where will it go?"[47]

Davids said, "The answer is that it will follow you."

By pulling instead of pushing, you create so much more clarity in the hearts and minds of your team. They see their goal more clearly and they see you, the leader, as an avenue to reach that goal. They spend less time worrying about the success of the mission and more time following you to the goal. Not only will you be more effective in reaching your

---

47 TEDxTalks. "The Rarest Commodity Is Leadership without Ego: Bob Davids at TEDxESCP." *YouTube*, April 10 2012.

goal by pulling rather than pushing, but also you will develop a deeper, more trusting relationship with your team by being in the trenches with them.

However, how do you know those people want to go where you're leading them? How do you know they share the vision you've developed? How do you know the last link in the chain wants to be connected just as much as the second link?

You have to use what Davids calls the "Consensus Method," and if you think you're too young to create consensus, don't worry. Davids learned it when he was sixteen!

As a young man growing up in Venice, California, Davids was an avid surfer. He loved surfing and working so much that he took a job as a surfboard sander at the local surf shop just off the beach in Venice at age thirteen. Yeah, times were different back then. Over time, employees kept moving on and Davids kept staying. Eventually the finishers, foam shapers, and night crew all quit and each time, Davids was asked to fill in and he energetically accepted.

"Long story short, I ended up doing every job. After two and a half years, I was fifteen, and I became the manager."

"Wow, how did you find yourself as manager when you were fifteen?" I asked.

"The owner, movie star Cliff Robertson's son approached me and said, 'The manager quit. I need you to be the manager now. Are you eighteen?' I was a tall guy, six-foot-four, so I looked down at him and said, 'Of course.' But I was the youngest in the business. Some employees were triple my age and I did not feel comfortable giving orders."

Talk about a freshman on the Varsity team. Some of Davids' teammates were married and he couldn't even buy a beer across the street yet. So what did he do? He learned how to create action through simplicity and consensus. What he lacked in seniority, he compensated for in the ability to create shared vision without groupthink.

"So I developed this framework where instead of commanding people, I would just talk with them about what needed to be done. My whole goal was to guide them toward an answer and create consensus."

Davids did not tell his people why his decisions and strategy were best. Rather, he invited them into the decision-making process and allowed them to own a share of the vision because he knew people with equity in the mission would perform even better. Furthermore, he protected against complacency and groupthink by continuously asking questions.

"If you don't get the right answer about the problem, you just ask the question again differently. And this is the beginning of pulling versus pushing because you can pull someone by just changing the question. This was the genesis of trying to lead by consensus because in doing so people will open the door to your vision."

Lead by consensus, not orders because people will work, grind, and overcome hardship for a consensus, but not for an order. People can be pushed only so far, but true success and excellence arise when teams are pulled toward the goal. Davids learned the power of pulling through consensus when he was sixteen, and six successful companies, a winery, and a resort later, the principle is still true. Value people by pulling them with you toward the goal.

Parenting and leadership are two sides of the same coin. Parents have to pull their children toward the goal of becoming adults. Although sometimes it can be too much pushing. How many of you have heard the age-old phrase from your parents: "Because I said so!" I imagine many of you have and if you're like me, it always infuriated you.

For one thing, people do not like being told to do something. Furthermore, people especially do not like being told to do something that they do not believe in or understand why they are doing it in the first place. Simply put, when people are pulled toward their goal and understand the why behind their mission, they are far more likely to approach the task with enthusiasm and determination, even if the task is unpleasant or difficult.

My mom always told me growing up: "You have to get good grades. You must do your best in school!"

I heard that lesson so much that it was more of a comma than an occasional message growing up. I was a well-behaved boy and I followed her instructions, but only because she told me to, not because I truly understood the significance behind investing in myself.

As I became older, she began to make it more clear to me what studying and applying myself would do. She talked about how her mother ran out of money for college in her sophomore year, but eventually finished her degree years later in a time when few women graduated from college. She earned enough money to send my mom to college who now proudly sits atop three degrees with two kids of her own in college. She stopped pushing me toward my goal with orders and instead starting pulling me toward the goal of being a responsible, educated adult, using her example.

Leadership is the exact same phenomenon. Leaders get the most out of their team members when they pull them through to the objective using the power of why. Oftentimes, this practice requires extra effort on the part of the leader, but it's the foundation of incredible team success. Management is about pushing the team toward the goal. Leadership is about connecting your people to the mission behind their objective and pulling the team through to that objective. Management relies on control and certitude. Leadership relies on inspiration and encouragement. A manager can command people, but they cannot influence and inspire people. Commanded people don't produce record results. Inspired people rewrite the record books.

One of the questions I received most often in this project was how college students can ascend the ladder and become leaders—as if a secret sauce propels some up the ladder more quickly than others. For one thing, some people are just more gifted than others and find themselves being promoted quickly for their unique talents. But bear in mind that those talents don't automatically translate into leadership or immediate success.

The example I like to give is LeBron James. He catapulted from Notre Dame into the NBA, but he wasn't a leader because of his dunks, three pointers, or defense. Those things made him talented, but not necessarily a leader. His teammates bestowed leadership on him over time for his daily accountability, and vision—his self-leadership. In other words, he did not pursue leadership. Leadership ensued from his conduct.

The more you aim for leadership, the clearer it becomes that you desire it for the wrong reasons. The more you aim for leadership, the more you are aiming for the opportunity to push people and feed your ego, not lead by example. Your people have to put you into leadership and link onto you as the first link in the chain because they see you doing whatever it takes to make the organization succeed, not whatever it takes to become CEO.

As Davids further explained to me, "Great leaders get put into positions of leadership by their people because they walk in their teammates' shoes. They don't have an ego, they're willing to do the dirtiest jobs, and they're willing to contribute in any way they can to the effort of that team."

I don't have any special sauce to get you from commencement to the C-Suite, but I have a couple of suggestions. First, stop aiming for leadership and start focusing on exceeding expectations in your role. Focus on excellence in whatever role you occupy and the recognition and position will follow. People make someone a leader because they go above and beyond and focus on achieving excellence, not because they're senior or tenured.

Second, lose any sense of ego in your organization or role. Instead, replace your ego with the reputation and success of your organization. In other words, stop thinking about your ego and start thinking about winning. If doing the toughest job no one else wants to do means your organization benefits, be the first one to take that job. If you're the one always volunteering for the challenging, frustrating, or otherwise ego-draining tasks, your teammates will notice and you'll find yourself in a position of leadership sooner than you might think.

Davids lives by the best advice on eliminating ego in his leadership roles:

"If you think you're special, you're not. If you know you're not special, you are."

CHAPTER 9

LIVE YOUR VALUES

"You create a new standard every time you decide to push a little further."

—MICHAEL TEOH, FOUNDER OF THRIVING TALENTS

During my research for this project, I had the opportunity to interview Mr. James Rosebush, who is a former senior aide to President Ronald Reagan, former Chief of Staff to Nancy Reagan, and former Director of Private Sector Initiatives in the Reagan administration. He has since served on the boards of many nonprofits and companies, and he now leads his own wealth management business. Having served in three senior roles in the Reagan White House, the Reagans became his best friends. Furthermore, Jim became extremely well-acquainted with their leadership, which inspired confidence in America at a time when it seemed like faith in America might be waning.

But Jim's story is unique. Jim didn't work on Reagan's campaign. He had no understanding of Reagan's leadership outside of what one would see on the TV during the campaign. He heard Reagan's words, but he didn't understand the voice from which they were spoken. In short, he knew Reagan the politician, but he didn't know Reagan the man. But when offered the job as Director of Private Sector Initiatives, Jim took the role without a hint of hesitation. Who turns down a chance to lead one of the president's favorite initiatives and be a senior aide to the president? And so in the spring of 1981, Jim joined President Reagan's newly inaugurated administration. Jim's job was to find ways for the private sector to partner with the federal government to more efficiently spend taxpayer money in government outlays.

On this particular morning, the president was to make a speech before various congressional leaders regarding the points of his plan and how he could enlist congressional support for the initiative.

On that brisk morning in Washington, D.C., President Reagan and Jim both strode toward "The Beast," the president's limousine complete with eight-inch armored doors, bulletproof glass, and three Secret Service agents. Secret Service walked them down the South Lawn toward the mammoth limousine. The door shut and suddenly, President Reagan and Jim were sitting next to each other in the backseat of the most important limousine in the world. Jim was about to get his first real taste of Reagan, the leader, rather than just Reagan the politician.

Just like practically every aide and advisor in this young administration, Jim was doing his best to prove his place in the White House and make his face time with the president count. He had prepared a long, extensive report on how the administration planned to use the private sector to improve government services for the American people. Jim began his brief, citing multiple projects and the contingencies associated with them. Jim then moved to the speech the president was to give, highlighting the various points of the plan that needed to be emphasized that day.

However, Jim soon realized that the president was not exactly listening. Rather, Reagan was looking out of the window at the motorcade and police escort spanning down Pennsylvania Avenue. He was taking in the amazing scene that is downtown DC. His next words astonished Jim.[48]

"Jim, did I ever tell you about my mother?"

---

48 James Rosebush, "From a Ride in Ronald Reagan's Limo, Lessons on Authenticity," *Christian Science Monitor*. May 16 2012.

Jim was stunned. He had absolutely no idea what to say. He had spent so much time preparing for one of the president's most prized initiatives and an important speech the president needed to give perfectly early on in his administration, yet he chose to ask Jim if he had talked about his mother? Jim finally got around to saying:

"No, Mr. President. You never told me about your mother."

The President responded, "My mother taught me all of my values from a very young age."

The president then continued, detailing how Nelle Reagan had taught him the values of seeing the good in people and valuing their virtues over their vices. As a preacher and minister, Nelle Reagan was the source of President Reagan's values. Ronald Reagan was scarred by his alcoholic father, Jack Reagan, but he gained self-confidence and leadership abilities through the values Nelle transmitted to him through the Bible, values that would propel him to the highest office in the land.

Jim was still stunned, but he was beginning to understand. Writing about the incident later, Jim realized that "Americans responded well to Reagan telling them they were part of a grand experiment to benefit the world."

In other words, people followed Reagan because he lived his values of affirming his people and recognizing their worth.

Not only did President Reagan live his values, but also he had the awareness to know that this was Jim's first glimpse at him as the new leader for whom he would be working. It was an extremely intimate moment, and President Reagan knew that what Jim needed most in this early stage was Reagan's value proposition. Why follow me? Why work for me in this administration? One of our greatest presidents understood it best. Your values are your navigation, and people must be able to see them front and center. President Reagan was such an effective leader because he found a way to connect his character to leadership.

Jim was so moved by Nancy and Ronald Reagan's value system in his five years in the White House that he refers to those years as the best of his life. In fact, Jim has written one of the bestselling books on Ronald Reagan, *True Reagan*, yet he admits frequently that many other people knew President Reagan much better than he did. Then how does Jim understand Reagan's leadership so well? Because he knew Reagan's values. He learned the moral structure behind the way Reagan's leadership operated: his value system that he held sacred.

Why do people need to see your values as a leader? When people see your values, they make a conscious choice about how willing they are to follow you, especially in a time of crisis. We want to follow people who make us feel safe, supported, and confident regardless of the situation. Everyone knows you can pilot in fair winds and calm seas, but they want an understanding of how you'll lead when crises arise and storms hit. They want an expectation of effective leadership when it all goes wrong. People look for and connect to your values because they know they are the foundation on which you will lead your team regardless of circumstance.

So how do you showcase your values as a leader and connect them to the hearts of your team? The way you do this is to take the leader out of the showroom, remove the bells and whistles, turn off the show lights, and open up the hood. That's what President Reagan did with Jim in the back of the Beast that morning in 1981. He presented Jim with a deep look into his values and character, understanding that those qualities would inspire Jim to lead in their administration.

One of the responses I hear most often about values in leadership is that some leaders are trusted for their seniority, knowledge, and experience more than their values. This is a fair comment, but it's important to reevaluate what underlies seniority, knowledge, and experience. Those three things are what values are built on! You develop your values from the experiences you've had, both positive and negative, until you find what you believe creates the most success. Your values determine your worth far more than your age or seniority in leadership roles. Find me an entry-level employee not in a traditionally understood leadership role who is actively refining their values and working to employ them, and you have found yourself a leader.

Michael Teoh is one such leader. Michael founded one of the most successful consulting businesses in Malaysia, Thriving Talents. Thriving Talents specializes in helping companies develop the leadership skills of their millennial talent as they prepare to enter leadership roles. His firm's services have been sought after by many Fortune 500 companies, including Microsoft, Deloitte, HSBC, and GE. Michael has even hosted former US President Barack Obama and Malaysian Prime Minister Najib Razak at his workshops for millennial leaders in Malaysia. I like to call Thriving Talents the McKinsey of Malaysia.

Oh, by the way, Michael is thirty and his business is only six years old.

How did Michael do this? Why have so many people signed on to follow him and work with him? Why have so many companies enlisted his help to develop young leaders and get the most out of their millennial talent? Michael did it through his values. Early on, Thriving Talents had little on which to run. They were a young firm, and acquiring clients was a challenge. In fact, the first time Michael offered his services to a friend, he was greeted with laughter. But this was also his proudest leadership moment because when his company got knocked down, it fell down on and rebuilt from its values.

"I've always been a believer that your values must become your compass as a leader during daunting moments or the most challenging times. Trust me, when I started Thriving Talents at the tender age of twenty-four and when we approached our first few clients, they laughed me out of the office. They would say, 'Michael, my kids are older than you, yet you're here trying to get me to hire you? Are you out of your mind?'"

But Michael's three core values are trust, loyalty, and collaboration, all three of which catapulted Thriving Talents to remarkable success. Michael showed he was here for the team and their great purpose, developing young employees into the leaders he knew they could be. Michael did whatever it took, neglecting salary and becoming the well from which his teammates drew their inspiration.

Trust could never have been stronger even as they struggled to find clients. That trust led to loyalty, and Michael was more loyal to the company than a captain is to his ship. He lived loyalty just like Patrick Lee did at Rotten Tomatoes and that example permeated the organization. Finally, he relied on collaboration—involving his teammates in the creative process for developing training programs to sell to companies. After months of rejection, Michael remained his team's well and his loyalty was rewarded as Microsoft offered them a consulting contract to train their new hires into effective leaders. The rest of the story is history. After successful services with Microsoft and GE, famous leaders from President Obama to Sir Richard Branson turned out to hear what Thriving Talents had to say about leadership development.

While Michael's story is not to say that trust, loyalty, and collaboration are the only values an organization needs, the important lesson is that living your values compounds on itself. The majority of the growth in Thriving Talents occurred toward the end of their painful start-up stage when clients were tough to come by. In the time when it was most painful to stay loyal, trust teammates, and collaborate, those three values did the most wonder for the company. Most importantly, those values and that success came from the inspiration of the leader, Michael, living them day in and day out even though he was so young and under so much pressure.

The final point that today's young leaders should be aware of regarding values is the importance of circulating and celebrating their effect throughout the organization. How often do you hear about your business's values? Quite often, I'm assuming. But, how often do you actually see those values being put into place in a measurable way in a company or organization? I'm guessing not as often. This is exactly why it's integral for leaders to archive stories and examples of their company and employees living their values to reinforce their impact on people, the bottom line, and their greater purpose.

During this project, I had a chance to interview a serial entrepreneur who ran an airline ticketing business. He told me the remarkable story of how he learned to celebrate and reinforce values not because it sounds altruistic, but because it encourages teammates to keep improving the company by living those values. Their main value at the company is "people over profits" and not only did it save the company, but it also made it one of the most profitable in its industry.

One day, this man walked into the office to learn that their largest contract had been terminated because of an internal mistake handling privacy. The client was furious and needless to say, it was a major setback for this man and his business.

However, he received another call a few weeks later.

"We'd like to resign our contract and actually we'll double our services, please."

Interesting, right? How did we go from terminating our largest client to doubling their account size?

As it turns out, a certain employee was living out "people over profits" better than anyone else. As this man was soon to find out, an account manager who wasn't even on this account answered the call from the furious client, learned she was having some serious family trouble, and began babysitting her children after work even though their relationship with this client had been severed.

The client explained, "We understand how much your people mean to you and we're proud to do business with a company that values its people so much. We'd like to double our account and resign our contract."

Priceline.com is now worth hundreds of millions of dollars and Jeff Hoffman is one of the most successful entrepreneurs in business. But notice, this success didn't come about because of some special talent, superman heroics, or divine wisdom. It arose because everyone in Jeff's company understood how their values drive their greater purpose and they committed to them because Jeff committed to them.

Jeff committed to his people so much that not a single employee left Priceline.com from the day it was founded until the day it was sold. How often do we hear about a situation like that? People didn't leave because Jeff lived his value of supporting people. One of his first employees used to live in a trailer park in Florida and when he was hired at Priceline.com, Jeff asked him how Priceline.com could help him achieve his personal goals. The man answered his long term goal is to have enough money to help his mom live in a safe neighborhood in her own home. Jeff never forgot that request and granted this man equity in the company as he did with all employees. Years later, after Jeff and his team built a remarkable, valuable company, he helped his good friend and longtime employee move his mother into her new home. It was his proudest leadership moment and one in which he shed more than a few tears because he knew he was living his values.

Leaders, as we said, are the symbol of an organization. They represent everything the company or unit stands for. They are the what, the how, and most importantly, the why. Above all else, leaders are the embodiment of an organization's values. Values are the most important tool we have in life because they are navigational at their core. You organize your life around your values just as you organize your house around the foundation and support beams. Live your values and they will give your organization abundant life and direction no matter the circumstances.

CHAPTER 10

VULNERABILITY

"I have been accused of making my subordinates my equals, and I happily stand guilty."

—USMC GENERAL AND SECRETARY OF DEFENSE JAMES MATTIS

Vulnerability is not often associated with leadership in popular understandings. In fact, if you ask most people, they would probably agree that vulnerability is more descriptive of followers than leaders. Leaders shouldn't act vulnerable. They're heroes. This is the classic myth of leaders being heroes and not real people. But what would you do if I told you that vulnerability, properly employed, is a key trait of an effective leader?

This is because vulnerability leads to trust. In fact, trust is just the "willingness to be vulnerable."[49] We trust people who we can count on to be comfortable when crises arise. Now, vulnerability is not walking around sharing every detail of your life, but rather being an honest individual who is comfortable with the hurdles one faces in life. Leaders who are being vulnerable in times of challenge are just being comfortable in who they are despite what is going on around them. Vulnerable leaders are content not having all the answers, being the smartest in the room, or being perfect.

Doesn't that undermine your leadership, though? If you're not the best, smartest, or perfect all the time, why should you be leading instead of someone else? You are worth following even though you are not perfect because you exhibit the comfortability being vulnerable. Everyone can lead in calm seas, but it's how leaders conduct themselves in time of challenge and change that makes them extraordinary. Vulnerability is what drives success in hard times because your example of vulnerability grants your teammates the permission to be vulnerable too. As your example goes, your teammates follow. The more transparent and vulnerable you are in trying times, the more confident your teammates will

49 Roger Mayer, James Davis, and David Schoorman, "An Integrative Model of Organizational Trust," *Academy of Management Review* Vol. 20, No. 3. (July 1995), 712.

be in maintaining authenticity and vulnerability when the pressure is on the team.

Right next to compassion in the leadership aisle is vulnerability. We have already learned that leaders must be connected to their teams on an emotional level through their vision and servant leadership. However, how easy is it to connect to someone who seems super human and unrelatable? Leaders need to make a concerted effort to show that they are real people just like their team. Not only does this allow them to better relate to their leader, but also it gives your people permission to be themselves too. No one feels like they need to hide behind a facade when authenticity is embraced by the leader of a team. As Kerry Bunker, founder of Mangrove Leadership Solutions and Senior Fellow at the Center for Creative Leadership, believes, "Personal vulnerability opens the door to helping others, but the truth is that most leaders wear protective masks that they don't remove easily or lightly."[50] In other words, embracing vulnerability allows people to feel comfortable not hiding behind a facade and holding in their emotions.

How often have you thought of leadership and immediately images of perfection, courage, and strength enter your mind? I imagine the word "vulnerability" was not the first thing

50 Kerry Bunker, "The Power of Vulnerability in Contemporary Leadership," *Consulting Psychology Journal* Vol. 49 (Spring 1997), 122-136.

that entered your mind. So often we see movies, TV shows, and books illustrate leaders as the absolute, impeccable individuals we should all strive to emulate. They seem to never be phased by pain or stress, just bearing it in stride as the model for leadership. Hardship seems to never find their plate and even when it does, they find ways to endure. But how authentic is that image? Have you ever met someone who is "perfect" or doesn't feel stress? Leadership is about establishing a trusting, empowering relationship between leader and teammate. Relationships are formed from the ability to connect to someone else's experience, hopes, and fears. How are we to connect to someone who is seemingly larger than life?

Karin Hurt is the Founder and CEO of Let's Grow Leaders, an international leadership consulting firm. In observing and speaking to business executives, she finds the pervasive "tendency to always appear executive-like" without showing the human, vulnerable side of themselves to which people can connect. Whenever the floor is theirs, they choose to tell their stories of overcoming challenges and setbacks to achieve success.

They do this in an effort to justify their status as leaders, and there is merit to that given the road one must travel to become an executive in the business world. However, people tend to tune out success stories because they've heard all of these messages before: plan your work then work your plan, stay disciplined, network, relationships matter, work as a team, find the solution.

Interestingly, we learn most from stories that revolve around failure. We are more likely to listen to someone's story if they are discussing a time they faced failure because it shines them in a human light, allowing us to better understand their experience and trust them. But when was the last time you heard a big shot executive tell you about the time they missed a deadline, set unclear expectations, or disappointed their manager?

They rarely do it because everyone, especially leaders, wants to come across as Superman or Wonder Woman. But team members connect with these leaders the least. They may appear executive, trustworthy, and infallible, but they will fall short of true team excellence and commitment because they fail to show the human side of their leadership.

Before starting her leadership consulting business, Karin learned this lesson as an executive at Verizon. She spent sixteen years working at Verizon, including eleven years as an executive in human resources, sales, and operations. When she entered her role as Head of Customer Service, she had a particularly interesting meeting with her boss.

Her boss brought her in for a meeting in her second week on the job and asked her a deeply troubling question.

"Karin, I have a scorecard here and I want you to tell me which things you think you will fail at on this list."

The list included certain items like communication with management and certain performance metrics like customer service call ratings.

Karin had just come from HR and felt unconfident in her new roles leading all customer service operations. She saw this as a liability rather than an asset, and wanting to look executive-like in her new role, she responded with confidence: "Well, I'm not going to fail."

Her boss smiled and understood that Karin was not exactly getting the point of the exercise. She knew Karin would not be able to excel at every facet of the job. However, she wanted her to be prepared for failure in certain areas and to focus on the things she knew she could do well, the strengths for which she was selected for this key role.

"No one is perfect. Failure happens to everyone, so I just want to have a conversation about what you want to accomplish in this role and what is most important for your and our success."

Karin now understood what her boss was aiming for in this conversation. She wanted Karin to understand that she knew perfection was impossible and more importantly that perfection wasn't the standard at all. Oftentimes, when people come across as unauthentic and fail to be vulnerable, they do so because they are aiming for perfection instead of excellence. When you aim for perfection, people are unable to relate to you. People follow you because they want to be like you, but if you're trying to be perfect, how can they connect to you?

Instead, be open and honest about challenges you and your team face, and present the human side of you.

Vulnerability may seem counterproductive because people tend to assume leadership involves looking like you've always got everything figured out. Some people even claim that vulnerability works against self-leadership because it forces you to admit that you may not be positive, confident, and enthusiastic at all times.

But, I disagree with the notion that vulnerability hinders self-leadership because vulnerability breeds trust in times of severe crisis when trust is needed most. In fact, I see it as an integral display of self-awareness and self-confidence to be authentic and vulnerable with one's team. People who know they are led by a human being recognize that their leader has the capacity for empathy and self-awareness in the most trying of times. Even more importantly, they recognize that their leader will not abandon honesty and authenticity for the sake of their image in difficult times.

I had the opportunity to speak to Jess Ekstrom, the founder and CEO of Headbands of Hope. Headbands of Hope grew out of Jess's dual love of wearing headbands and her internship at the Make a Wish Foundation. For every headband that Headbands of Hope sells, the company donates a headband to the Four Diamonds Fund and $1 to the St. Baldrick's Foundation. It's a remarkable organization and one whose mission matches its purpose at every turn.

But the story wasn't always so bright.

Jess borrowed a significant amount of money from her family to start the business as a junior in college. The company secured orders and things were looking up, until they fell victim to a fake order. They spent all but a little of their cash reserves to produce the products for this sale when it was discovered too late that the order was fraudulent. All of a sudden, the company held loads of inventory with no buyer and little cash left over.

But Jess was honest with her team. She kept her composure, but she didn't put up a facade because she was comfortable being vulnerable. She certainly could have pointed fingers at a number of people, but she chose to own the mistake and be vulnerable. That decision to be calm in a time of vulnerability engendered deep-seated trust between Jess and her teammates. None of Jess's creditors or teammates abandoned faith in Jess even at this critical point in the venture because they recognized that she held a commitment to authenticity as a leader. Jess's honesty and vulnerability was soon rewarded as Headbands of Hope secured another creditor and a partner in their purpose of giving young cancer patients a headband even while they lost their hair.

Today, over a decade later, Headbands of Hope has proudly reached every single children's hospital in America and donated thousands of headbands to young cancer patients.

I know most of us will never face a crisis as dire as a Jess did, but the lesson is universal. Great leaders are not afraid to be vulnerable because they understand that honesty breeds trust. To inspire people, you must first connect with them and it's impossible to connect if you cloud yourself in inauthenticity. Vulnerability is not a sign of weakness, but of maturity, poise, and focus in times of trial. Nothing motivates people more in hard times than an authentic leader because they set the example for attitude when excuses are readily available.

CONCLUSION

"A person doing his or her best becomes a natural leader just by example."

—JOE DIMAGGIO

Leadership is just as much an art as it is a skill, and it can surely be a daunting task. One of the sentiments I hear most frequently from young leaders is "I didn't realize how hard leadership was until I was suddenly asked to lead." However, using the framework we have outlined in this book will help you conquer those fears by giving you a simple approach to growing your people and achieving remarkable results.

I encourage you to break the ten chapters of the book, the ten pillars of our leadership model, into three broad categories: You, Your People, and Your Purpose. This will allow you to focus on them one at a time as they build on one another. Let's be real, it would ridiculously difficult to achieve excellent self-leadership, establish a culture and vision, value your people and serve them, thrive on feedback, set the standard, and be transparent and disciplined all in one fell swoop.

In category 1, You, utilize chapters 1, 6, 7, and 10 to focus on developing your self-leadership through discipline, feedback, communication, and vulnerability. This category highlights how the way you conduct yourself provides the most concrete roadmap for your teammates to follow. The question you should always be using to guide yourself is how would I want my leader to approach this situation? Always set the example you would want to follow. We've all heard the Golden Rule, treat others how you want to be treated. The same principle applies here with self-leadership. Lead people how you would want to be led.

In category 2, Your People, utilize chapters 3, 4, and 5 to establish an effective culture that affirms, develops, and cares for your people. Remember, your people are your greatest asset and the more you invest in making them successful, the greater success you will all have as a team. Simon Sinek explained the importance of serving people as a leader best, "A weak leader likes to tell us how many people work for them. A great leader is humbled to tell us how many people they work for."

Finally, category 3, Your Purpose, includes chapters 2, 8, and 9 on vision, pulling vs. pushing, and living your values. Notice that category 3 is not about fulfilling your goal or mission, but fulfilling your purpose. We can accomplish many goals in our life time, but they may not align with our purpose. Invest the time to identify how your team's goal demonstrates your purpose just how Pat McClenahan did so well with the 2015 Special Olympics. Then, focus on pulling your team to the goal with your example and celebrate your people living the values of your team.

This is a process and one that takes significant investment to hone. If you think the price is too high or the learning curve too steep, consider this. You aren't honing your leadership skills for yourself. Rather, you are refining and improving your leadership ability because of your people, because their development and careers are on the line. Remember, this isn't about you, but who you are.

Remember how great leaders like Pat McClenahan and Coach Woodert find the vision, the inner why behind what their organization drives toward? I ask you to do the same thing here, just on a deeper, personal level. As you refine your leadership abilities, ask yourself on a daily basis what motivates you to do so. I promise if you think about other people—your coworkers, your parents, your children—those factors will motivate you to push further than if you use your own development as motivation to grow as a leader.

How much do you commit to being transparent, knowing your people, and focusing on their needs over your own? Is it an active component of your leadership or at the bottom of a long to-do list? As my mother would say, do you treat it as a trip to the dentist or a trip to the Dodger game? Undoubtedly, these practices take time and most leaders cite lack of time as a major impediment to accomplishing their agenda. However, if you incorporate the practice of discipline into your daily routine, you will experience tremendous growth in these areas over time. Jim Sinegal and Gregg Throgmartin are exceptional examples of disciplined leaders who go to extraordinary lengths to be in front of their people.

Jim Sinegal is the cofounder and former CEO of Costco, one of the largest, most successful wholesale retailer chains in the world. I hesitate to say that one leader makes the organization because as you've seen by now, leadership is about turning the focus toward your people and serving them, but Sinegal has left an indelible mark on Costco through his leadership. His approach was not all that revolutionary or groundbreaking. He valued his employees like family, checked his ego, and empowered people within the company to take on new roles and business opportunities. This sounds simple and not particularly awe-inspiring, right?

Then what allowed him to be CEO for twenty-seven years and create returns that beat the market handsomely over his nearly three-decade involvement with Costco? Discipline. The key is not only the conduct of Sinegal as a servant leader, but even more so the consistency and conviction with which he led as a servant.

When Sinegal was CEO of Costco, he would visit each of Costco's over seven hundred stores each year, spending two thirds of each year traveling around the world.[51] At every store he visited, he spent time with the employees and made a point to ask them how their work and lives were going at Costco.

Imagine hearing this question from the CEO of your company, a Fortune 500 company publicly traded on the Nasdaq: "How is work going here? What issues do you see with our business here at this location and how can we improve?"

---

51 Monica Soto Ouchi, "Getting a Lesson in Retail Inside World's Busiest Costco," The Seattle Times. July 15 2007.

Yet, this is the kind of question Sinegal would ask everyday employees as he bagged goods or refilled inventory with them on his visits.

Even in the depths of the Great Recession in 2008 when the global economy came to a screeching halt and many businesses, including Costco, began to suffer, Sinegal would not abandon his servant, compassionate, yet inspiring leadership framework. No one was laid off and wages remained at their historic Costco average of $20 per hour, the highest of the retail industry.

Layoffs are an unfortunate part of the business cycle and this isn't to say that if layoffs become absolutely necessary, one has abandoned servant leadership. When Costco expanded into unprofitable regions and had to close down, Sinegal took the same approach Patrick Lee did at Rotten Tomatoes. Furthermore, this example is also not meant to show that there's a simple formula to leadership success. Sinegal makes leadership look so easy even though there were many years of struggle and mistakes along the way.

The most important takeaway from Jim Sinegal and the remarkable story of Costco's success is the discipline with which he led with compassion and service. He wasn't just a servant leader at work. He lived it every day with a full understanding of how his example would be followed. The proof of how this works is the way Costco has operated in the six years since Sinegal's retirement in 2012. Management has continued Sinegal's legacy by treating employees well with exceptional pay and benefits and customers have continued to reward them by signing up for Costco memberships in record numbers.

I know I am asking you to do a lot. To be a self-leader, establish a vision and culture, serve your people, accept feedback and protect your brand all while listening to your people is difficult. Make no mistake about it, leadership is hard work. However, at the same time, I want us to think about how this process compounds on itself like compounding interest in your IRA. The more your people see you investing in your organization, your people, and their experience as Sinegal did all those years, the more people will connect to your self-leadership, vision, and culture.

Managers throughout Costco are so intrinsically motivated to perform well because they know their leader has them on his mind all the time. Simply, people chose to follow Sinegal because he earned it through his discipline as a leader and his return on investment in his people is one of the most successful companies of all time.

Gregg Throgmartin summed leadership up to me quite well:

"None of this stuff is particularly complicated or rocket science, Hunter. It just takes discipline and comfortability being uncomfortable. Most leaders don't want to go visit their store locations and interact with the people doing the hardest jobs in the company."

As simple as Gregg's words were, he was right. Hardly any of the leadership concepts I encountered in this nine month project were particularly complex or difficult to understand. However, the complexity arose in trying to understand how to do cover each of the 10 concepts in our model when time is limited. The secret is discipline. Once vision and culture have been set, discipline is the primary tool leaders need to employ to keep their teams on track by constantly setting a positive example, living the values of their organization, and pulling their teams toward the goal.

Dwight Eisenhower is most well known as the thirty-fourth President of the United States and the Supreme Commander of Allied Expeditionary Forces in Europe in World War II. However, what many people don't know about is Eisenhower's leadership approach in connecting with his soldiers. From December of 1943 to D-Day on June 6, 1944, the Allies planned Operation Overlord, their mission to break the Atlantic Wall and spell the beginning of the end of Nazi Germany. It would prove to be the most daring, complicated, and high stakes military operation in history, indeed a defining moment of the twentieth century. A total of 156,000 troops, 11,590 aircraft, 6,939 vessels, and 12 different nations would be involved, a massive logistical challenge that Eisenhower and his team spent months planning. [52]

Yet, Eisenhower always found the time to go visit the troops who were training for this historical mission. Troops from various Allied nations remarked how they consistently saw "the brass" walking around their bases in southwestern Britain in the months leading up to the operation.[53] Eisenhower remarked how he simply enjoyed hearing the stories of these individuals and their lives back home, separate from their service in the military.

Eisenhower knew soldiers of a foreign nation, especially the British, would not be as motivated to perform for him, an American general, unless he earned their trust. And so Eisenhower utilized discipline to constantly show the British, Canadians, and Australians who would carry out his orders that his leadership was worthy of following. When the order came to move out in the early morning hours of June 6, General Eisenhower had long since earned the trust of the Allied

52 "Figures of the Normandy Landings." *D-Day and Battle of Normandy Encyclopedia*.

53 Brian Clark, "Eisenhower's Leadership by Walking Around," Eisenhower's Leadership. September 14 2012.

soldiers by using discipline to show how seriously he took his job, their mission, and their lives.

I want us to think about this concept in terms of investment. Why would we go through all of the trouble of establishing a vision, culture, team, and servant leadership approach if we will just be undisciplined in putting it to its best use? Remember how vision, culture, and service compound on one another. Just think about the loss in performance sustained by not consistently communicating your reason for leading, your goal as the leader, and your commitment to your people beyond the role they play in accomplishing your mission. As General Eisenhower showed, being disciplined in implementing practices that gain trust and buy-in from your teammates should be the highlight of your day as visiting the troops was for him.

I know I've asked a lot of you in this book. But I hope you recognize that it is because I see tremendous value in my peers to lead our world. Not only do I see the value in us, but I see the need for our value in the world. I hope that I have spoken as much to your hearts as to your minds. It brings me immense joy and gratitude that your teams are benefiting from the lessons in this book. Never forget that leadership is about inspiring people, not inspiring your ego, and you will be impressed at how far your team goes. Leadership is a fine skill that takes time to develop and undoubtedly you will face roadblocks in your leadership journey. But remember, the potential of your team is at stake and nothing should matter more to a leader than his or her team.

May the leaders we are never meet the leaders we could have become.

Lead the way!

A COLLECTION OF IMPACTFUL LEADERSHIP QUOTES

"A good leader leads the people from above them. A great leader leads the people from within them."

—M.D. ARNOLD

"Leaders don't inflict pain. They share pain."

—MAX DE PREE

"Leadership is the art of giving people a platform for spreading ideas that work."

—SETH GODIN

"People ask the difference between a leader and a boss. The leader leads, and the boss drives."

—PRESIDENT THEODORE ROOSEVELT

"Treat people as if they were what they ought to be, and you help them become what they are capable of being."

—JOHANN WOLFGANG VON GOETHE

"The quality of a leader is reflected in the standards they set for themselves."

—RAY KROC

"Purpose affirms trust, trust affirms purpose, and together they forge individuals into a working team."

—GENERAL STANLEY MCCHRYSTAL

"The temptation to lead as a chess master, controlling each move of the organization, must give way to an approach as a gardener, enabling rather than directing."

—GENERAL STANLEY MCCHRYSTAL

"Customers will only love a company when the employees love it first."

—SIMON SINEK

"The supreme quality for leadership is unquestionably integrity. Without it, no real success is possible, no matter whether it is on a section gang, a football field, in an army, or in an office."

—US ARMY GENERAL AND 34TH PRESIDENT OF THE UNITED STATES DWIGHT EISENHOWER

"Motivation is the art of getting people to do what you want because they want to do it."

—US ARMY GENERAL AND 34TH PRESIDENT OF THE UNITED STATES DWIGHT EISENHOWER

"Leadership and learning are indispensable to each other."

—35TH PRESIDENT JOHN F. KENNEDY

"I am not afraid of an army of lions led by a sheep; I am afraid of an army of sheep led by a lion."

—ALEXANDER THE GREAT

"Leadership is practiced not so much in words as in attitudes and actions."

—HAROLD GENEEN FORMER PRESIDENT
AND CEO OF THE ITT COMPANY

"True leadership lies in guiding others to success—in ensuring that everyone is performing at their best, doing the work they are pledged to do and doing it well."

—BILL OWENS

"Wise leaders generally have wise counselors because it takes a wise person themselves to distinguish them."

—DIOGENES OF SINOPE

"Own 100 percent of your 50 percent of the blame."

—JIM SINEGAL, COFOUNDER AND FORMER CEO OF COSTCO

"If your actions inspire others to dream more, learn more, do more and become more, you are a leader."

—JOHN QUINCY ADAMS

"You don't lead by pointing and telling people some place to go. You lead by going to that place and making a case."

—KEN KESEY

"No man will make a great leader who wants to do it all himself, or to get all the credit for doing it."

—ANDREW CARNEGIE

"Outstanding leaders go out of their way to boost the self-esteem of their personnel. If people believe in themselves, it's amazing what they can accomplish."

—SAM WALTON

"Successful leaders see the opportunities in every difficulty rather than the difficulty in every opportunity."

—REED MARKHAM

"Leaders must be close enough to relate to others, but far enough ahead to motivate them."

—JOHN C. MAXWELL

"Leading people is the most challenging and, therefore, the most gratifying undertaking of all human endeavors."

—JOCKO WILLINK

"Don't tell people how to do things, tell them what to do and let them surprise you with their results."

—GEORGE PATTON

"A leader takes people where they want to go. A great leader takes people where they don't necessarily want to go but ought to be."

—ROSALYNN CARTER

"Failing organizations are usually over-managed and under-led."

—WARREN BENNIS

"A genuine leader is not a search of consensus, but a molder of consensus."

—DR. MARTIN LUTHER KING, JR.

"Leadership is not just about giving energy… it's unleashing other people's energy."

—PAUL POLMAN

"A weak leader likes to tell us how many people work for them. A great leader is humbled to tell us how many people they work for."

—SIMON SINEK

"Values are worthless until proven on the battlefield of life."

ACKNOWLEDGEMENTS

There are so many people who deserve thanks for their guidance, insight, feedback, and encouragement on this project. You all mean the world to me and your work and passion is as deeply embedded in these pages as mine.

First of all, thank you to Professor Eric Koester for giving me this opportunity to identify my passion, create a product around that passion, and share it with the world. You have been so generous to and supportive of me over the last year. I am eternally grateful for all that you have done for me and how much you have changed my life.

To my parents, thank you for your endless support. Mom and Dad, you've been the purest examples of leaders anyone could ever experience. I know I started the research for this project ten months ago, but believe me I've been watching and learning for over 21 years now.

To my wonderful sister, Evan. You inspire me with your positive attitude and work ethic every day. I cannot wait to see the incredible success you will create in your life and the remarkable people you will bring with you.

To all those who granted me their time and insight for interviews on this project, thank you for your generosity. This project would not have been possible without you and so many great leaders will benefit from the lessons you imparted on me.

To all those who read advanced copies of this book, thank you for your dedication to this project and your feedback. Your input provided invaluable perspective and contributed to the success of this book immensely.

To my classmates in Professor Koester's class, thank you for creating such a supportive, collaborative environment in which to write and explore our passions. I am so proud of all of us for staying the course on these projects and publishing our books. It's a monumental task of which we should all be incredibly proud. Even more importantly, let these books be proof that nothing is impossible in our lives if we are committed to ourselves and our passions.

To my friends and mentors at Georgetown University, thank you for all of your encouragement, support, and confidence. This was a team effort and I could never have done this without you all.

To my Sigma Chi brothers, thank you for your support along the way. This project challenged me in many ways, but you all inspired me to overcome those challenges. Continue developing as leaders, building the people around you with your gifts, and living lives of high ambition. May the men we are never meet the men we could have become.

God Bless

APPENDIX: BIBLIOGRAPHY

INTRODUCTION

Brack, Jessica and Kelly, Kip. "Maximizing Millennials in the Work Place," University of North Carolina Kenan-Flagler Business School: Executive Development. Accessed August 8 2018. https://www.kenan-flagler.unc.edu/executive-development/custom-programs/~/media/files/documents/executive-development/maximizing-millennials-in-the-workplace.pdf

Heimlich, Russell. "Baby Boomers Retire," Pew Research Center. Accessed August 6 2018. http://www.pewresearch.org/fact-tank/2010/12/29/baby-boomers-retire/

"State of Leadership Development 2015: The Time to Act is Now," Brandon Hall Group. Accessed 6 August 2018. http://www.brandonhall.com/mm5/merchant.mvc?Screen=PROD&Product_Code=IP15+-+State+of+Leadership+Development+2015

"The Millennial Leadership Survey." Workplace Trends. Accessed August 5 2018. https://workplacetrends.com/the-millennial-leadership-survey/

CHAPTER 1
SELF-LEADERSHIP

Jeter, Derek. "The Start of Something New." *The Player's Tribune.* October 1 2014. Accessed 8 August 2018.

Landrum, Sarah. "Millennials and the Resurgence of Emotional Intelligence," *Forbes.* Accessed October 2 2018.

CHAPTER 2
VISION

"Berlin Wall," The Ronald Reagan Presidential Library and Museum. Accessed 6 October 2018. https://www.reaganfoundation.org/library-museum/permanent-exhibitions/berlin-wall/

Deci, Edward. "The Effect of Contingent and Noncontingent Rewards and Controls on Intrinsic Motivation." *Organizational Behavior and Human Performance* 8 (1972): 217-229.

Dolan, Anthony. "Four Little Words," *The Wall Street Journal*, November 8 2009. https://www.wsj.com/articles/SB10001424052748704795604574522163362062796. Accessed August 11 2018.

Hawkins, Kirk. "Patrick McClenahan: Embracing the Spirit of Competition," *CSQ*, June 25 2015. https://csq.com/2015/08/patrick-mcclenahan-embracing-the-spirit-of-competition/#.W8JQUBNKi8p. Accessed July 26 2018.

"Michelle Obama and Jamaal Charles join Special Olympics Athletes at 2015 World Games Opening Ceremony," Special Olympics. https://www.specialolympics.org/stories/athletes/michelle-obama-and-jamaal-charles-join-special-olympics-athletes-at-2015-world-games-opening-ceremony. Accessed 6 August 2018.

"Obama vs. Romney: Election Eve Rallies," CNN Election Center. November 5 2012. Accessed 5 October 2018.

"Obama 2012," SS&K Advertising. https://www.ssk.com/work/work-obama.html. Accessed 7 October 2018.

Orzini, Cesar, Phillip Evans, and Oscar Jerez. "How to Encourage Intrinsic Motivation in the Clinical Teaching Environment? A Systematic Review from the Self-Determination Theory." *Journal of Educational Evaluation for Health Professionals* vol. 12, no. 8 (2015) https://doi.org/10.3352/jeehp.2015.12.8

Robinson, Peter. "'Tear Down This Wall': How Top Advisors Opposed Reagan's Challenge to Gorbachev-But Lost." *National Archives Prologue Magazine* Vol. 39, No. 2 (Summer 2007). https://www.archives.gov/publications/prologue/2007/summer/berlin.html. Accessed 7 October 2018.

"Special Olympics World Games CEO McClenahan Named Sports Executive of the Year," Fox Sports. https://www.foxsports.com/west/story/patrick-mcclenahan-special-olympics-world-games-ceo-named-2015-sports-executive-of-year-012016. Accessed July 28 2018.

Walsh, Kenneth. "Seizing the Moment: Memorable Presidential Speeches are Few and Far Between. But Ronald Reagan's Words in Berlin Two Decades Ago Will Live On." US News and World Report. https://web.archive.org/web/20070614042154/http://www.usnews.com/usnews/news/articles/070610/18speeches.htm. Accessed 2 October 2018.

CHAPTER 3
VISION

McCafferty, Dennis. "The Top 10 CEOs at US Tech Companies," *Baseline*, April 8 2014. http://www.baselinemag.com/it-management/slideshows/the-top-ten-ceos-at-u.s.-tech-companies.html?kc=EWKNLEND04122014STR2&dni=118567836&rni=22932983. Accessed 13 August 2018.

"Only in Hollywood," Sportsnet LA. July 15 2018.

Tom Roeder, "James Mattis Tells Air Force Graduating Class: 'Your Primary Weapon Now is Your Attitude," *The Gazette*, May 23 2018. https://gazette.com/military/james-mattis-tells-air-force-academy-graduating-class-your-primary/article_b7a801d8-ab57-5eac-ac1a-efa50db143df.html. Accessed 10 October 2018.

Weiner, Jeff. "Jeff Weiner on Establishing a Culture and a Plan for Scaling." Lynda.com. January 17 2017. Accessed 3 August 2018.

CHAPTER 4
PEOPLE

Alden, Chris. "Looking Back on the Crash," *The Guardian*, March 10 2005. https://www.theguardian.com/technology/2005/mar/10/newmedia.media. Accessed 28 September 2018.

Boitnott, John. "7 Leadership Lessons from U.S. Secretary of Defense James Mattis," *Entrepreneur*, March 6 2018. https://www.entrepreneur.com/article/309654. Accessed 12 April 2018.

Davis, Marc. "How September 11th Affected the Stock Market," Investopedia. https://www.investopedia.com/financial-edge/0911/how-september-11-affected-the-u.s.-stock-market.aspx. Accessed 8 October 2018.

Lefton, Terry. "Everyone Trusts Joe." *Sports Business Journal*, March 7 2016. https://www.sportsbusinessdaily.com/Journal/Issues/2016/03/07/Champions/Cohen.aspx. Accessed July 26 2018.

Nemo, John. "What a NASA Janitor Can Teach Us About Living a Bigger Life." *The Business Journals*, December 23 2014. https://www.bizjournals.com/bizjournals/how-to/growth-strategies/2014/12/what-a-nasa-janitor-can-teach-us.html. Accessed 3 August 2018.

Owens, Bradley and David Hekman, "How Does Leader Humility Influence Team Performance? Exploring the Mechanisms of Contagion and Collective Promotion Focus," *Academy of Management Journal* Vol. 59, no. 3 (2016): 1088-1111.

Ryan, Tim. "Rotten Tomatoes Oral History." Rotten Tomatoes. December 4 2009.

Sue Shellenbarger, "The Best Bosses Are Humble Bosses," *The Wall Street Journal*, October 9 2018. https://www.wsj.com/articles/the-best-bosses-are-humble-bosses-1539092123. Accessed October 9 2018.

Bill Snyder, "Mastercard CEO: Challenge Conventional Wisdom," Stanford Business School. https://www.gsb.stanford.edu/insights/mastercard-ceo-challenge-conventional-wisdom. Accessed 14 September 2018.

Wartzman, Rick and Lawrence Cosby, "A Company's Performance Depends First of All on Its People," *The Wall Street Journal*, August 12 2018. https://www.wsj.com/articles/a-companys-performance-depends-first-of-all-on-its-people-1534125840. Accessed 13 August 2018.

Zhou, Jinyi and Yawen Li. "The Role of Leader's Humility in Facilitating FrontlineEmployees' Deep Acting and Turnover: The Moderating Role of Perceived Customer-Oriented Climate." *Journal of Leadership and Organizational Studies*. Vol. 25, no. 3 (2018): 353-367.

CHAPTER 5
SERVE

Chris Graythen, "Drew Brees Breaks All-Time Passing Yard Record." CBS News. October 9 2018. https://www.cbsnews.com/

news/drew-brees-all-time-passing-yard-record-new-orleans-saints-nfl-today-2018-10-08/. Accessed 10 October 2018.

CHAPTER 6
FEEDBACK

"History of Godiva," Godiva Chocolatier. September 18 2007.

"Ulker Group to Buy Campbell's Godiva." Just-Food. December 21 2007. https://www.just-food.com/news/%C3%BClker-group-to-buy-campbells-godiva_id100748.aspx. Accessed 20 July 2018.

CHAPTER 8
DON'T PUSH, PULL

Burrows, Dan. "Mattel Buys Radica for $230 Million." Market Watch. July 26 2006. https://www.marketwatch.com/story/mattel-buys-radica-games-for-230-mln-in-cash. Accessed 12 September 2018.

Davids, Bob. "The Rarest Commodity Is Leadership without Ego: Bob Davids at TEDxESCP." *YouTube*, April 10 2012. https://www.youtube.com/watch?v=UQrPVmcgJJk. Accessed 21 March 2018.

CHAPTER 9
LIVE YOUR VALUES

Rosebush, James. "From a Ride in Ronald Reagan's Limo, Lessons on Authenticity." *Christian Science Monitor.* May 16 2012. https://www.csmonitor.com/Commentary/Opinion/2012/0516/From-a-ride-in-Ronald-Reagan-s-limo-lessons-on-authenticity. Accessed 9 May 2018.

CHAPTER 10
VULNERABILITY

Bunker, Kerry. "The Power of Vulnerability in Contemporary Leadership." *Consulting Psychology Journal* Vol. 49 (Spring 1997), 122-136.

Mayer, Roger, James Davis, and David Schoorman, "An Integrative Model of Organizational Trust." *Academy of Management Review* Vol. 20, No. 3. (July 1995), 712.

CONCLUSION

Clark, Brian. "Eisenhower's Leadership by Walking Around." Eisenhower's Leadership, September 14 2012. https://eisenhowersleadership.com/2012/09/14/eisnhower-leadership-by-walking-around/. Accessed 13 September 2018.

"Figures of the Normandy Landings." *D-Day and Battle of Normandy Encyclopedia.* https://www.dday-overlord.com/en/d-day/figures. Accessed 1 October 2018.

Soto Ouchi, Monica. "Getting a Lesson in Retail Inside World's Busiest Costco." *The Seattle Times*, July 15 2007. http://old.seattletimes.com/html/businesstechnology/2003790031_costcohawaii15.html. Accessed 8 July 2018.